**EDUCATION INSIDE THE
LIBRARY-MEDIA CENTER**

education
inside
the
library-media
center

Richard W. Hostrop

LINNET BOOKS   1973

Library of Congress Cataloging in Publication Data

Hostrop, Richard W.
  Education inside the library-media center.

  Bibliography: p.
  1. Instructional materials centers. 2. Libraries and students.
I. Title.
LB3044.H67   027.7   72-13425
ISBN 0-208-01324-5

To:

B. Lamar Johnson, who taught me about books—and more.

F. Dean McCluskey, who taught me about "nonbooks"—and more.

Louis Shores, who taught me about the *Generic Book*—and more.

CONTENTS

ILLUSTRATIONS

TABLES

PREFACE

EDUCATION INSIDE THE LIBRARY-MEDIA CENTER begins with a discussion of the foundation upon which the modern learning center rests. The teaching ⇔ learning role of the merged print/nonprint center is explored in subsequent chapters—beginning with the elementary school and concluding with the university. A look at the Library-College concept and the future of Library-Media Centers (L-MCs) concludes this work.

Relevant research findings, many of which have never before been reported, permeate the chapters. The findings from several in-depth studies suggest the need for, and ways to achieve, "putting education inside the L-MC" so as to achieve more effective student learning. Analysis of findings from several breadth studies suggest certain L-MC changes which can result in maximizing the effectiveness of limited funds available.

EDUCATION INSIDE THE LIBRARY-MEDIA CENTER has been written to serve as a textbook for aspiring educational librarians and technologists. It also has been written to serve as an aid to practicing educational librarians and technologists who sense the urgency of providing learners with a unified materials approach.

Homewood, Illinois   Richard W. Hostrop

ACKNOWLEDGMENTS

Though the contents of this work are my responsibility alone, I wish to publicly acknowledge my appreciation for the valuable suggestions made by the following who critically reviewed various portions of the manuscript during its developmental stage:

Robert Baker, Howard Clayton, George Fox, Peggy Hall, LeeOna Hostrop, Father Edward Lamorte, Carol Obriecht, Allene Schnaitter, Louis Shores, and Richard Vorwerk.

EDUCATION INSIDE THE
LIBRARY-MEDIA CENTER

A LOOK BACKWARDS

The art of writing is the mother of orators and the father of artists—Sumerian Proverb

Before media centers could be established, nonprint technological instructional aids had to be developed. Before libraries could be established, "books" had to be written. But before books could be written man had to learn how to write. Thus the beginnings of today's library-media centers must be traced back to the earliest beginnings of writing more than 5,000 years ago.

Writing

Of the many contributions of Mesopotamia (the ancient country between the Tigris and Euphrates rivers) to the progress of mankind, no other can compare in importance with the introduction of writing to the world. The idea of writing was first developed in southern Mesopotamia among the Sumerians who had a strong sense of private property. They used the cylinder seal to mark and identify their property in the temple, and for economic purposes.

Soon other peoples developed (either independently or through contact with the Sumerians), and were using, early forms of writing. Development was along two principal lines: Mesopotamian cuneiform (the wedge-shaped characters used in ancient Sumerian, Akkadian, Assyrian, Babylonian, and Persian writing)—e.g.

and Egyptian hieroglyphics (a system of writing in which figures or objects are used to represent words or sounds)—e.g.

Egyptian writing appeared after the Sumerians had perfected their medium; as far as we know, it lacked the preliminary experimental stage being fully developed virtually from the moment of its appearance. Egypt and Mesopotamia are known to have maintained close cultural contacts with each other in the centuries prior to the advent of writing, and the idea of writing could have been readily communicated from one to the other. Some scholars now agree that Egypt took over the basic idea from Mesopotamia, but employed its own specific symbols to put the idea into effect.

The development of written language progressed from the expression of names to the expression of words and sentences and further to the expression of component syllables, the development proceeding from the concrete to the abstract. The development of syllables marked a liberation from mere word painting.

Even though the idea of writing had become accepted and used, it required more than 1,000 years before the next great stride was taken—this time from syllabic to alphabetic writing. The development of alphabetic writing was also a contribution of the near East, probably of the Palestinians and Syrians. However, it was the Greeks who adapted and stabilized the alphabet as an instrument of communication, especially verbal communication. The written alphabet, as known today in western civilizations, is that developed by the Romans. Originally adapted from the early form of an Etruscan alphabet for writing Latin, it had only twenty or twenty-one letters to begin with, but by the Medieval Latin period had twenty-six letters. It is today the most extensively used of all the world's alphabets.

Books

How soon after the invention of writing men began to make books as we know them is difficult to ascertain. It is generally believed that the oldest extant examples of writing are on stone. The earliest known "books" were the clay tablets of Mesopotamia and the papyrus rolls of Egypt. Examples of both date from the early third millennium B.C.

The ancient Sumerians, Babylonians, Assyrians and Hittites wrote on tablets made from water-cleaned clay. Although these writing bricks varied in shape and dimensions, a common form was a tetrahedron about five inches long. While the clay was still wet, the writer used a stylus to inscribe it with cuneiform characters. By writing on every surface in small characters, he could copy a substantial text on a single tablet. For longer texts he used several tablets, linking them together by numbers and catch-words as is done in modern books.

The papyrus roll of ancient Egypt is more nearly the direct ancestor of the modern book than is the clay tablet, and it is almost as ancient. Papyrus as a writing material resembles paper. It was made from a reedy plant of the same name which flourished in the Nile Valley. Strips of papyrus pith laid at right angles on top of each other and pasted together made cream colored papery sheets. Although the sheets varied in size, ordinary ones measured about five to six inches wide. The sheets were pasted together at alternate edges to make a long roll. To make a book, the scribe copied a text on the side of the sheets where the strips of pith ran horizontally, and the finished product was rolled up with the text inside. Compared to clay tablets, papyrus is fragile, yet an example exists dating back to 2500 B.C.; and older stone inscriptions portray scribes with rolls.

Archeological evidence indicates that the Chinese had writing and probably books at least as early as 1300 B.C. These early primitive books were made of wood or bamboo strips bound together with cords. Many such books were burned by the Chinese in 213 B.C. at the time Emperor Shih Huany Ti reigned. The fragility of materials and the damp climate resulted in the loss of other ancient copies.

The Greeks adapted the papyrus roll and passed it on to the Romans. Although both Greeks and Romans used other writing materials (waxed wooden tablets, for example) the Greek and Roman words for book show identification with the Egyptian model. Greek *biblion* ("book") can be compared with byblos ("papyrus"), while the Latin *volumen* ("book") signified a roll.

Except for the substitution of the Latin alphabet, a Roman papyrus roll closely resembled a Greek one in content. But the Romans evidently developed a book trade on a fairly large scale. From the time of Cicero there is evidence of large scriptoria turning out copies of books for sale. On several occasions Cicero referred to book shops. Martial complained about professional copyists who became careless in their speed; Pliny described the extensive trade in papyrus. The trade decrees of Diocletian set a price for the copying of books.

Book ownership was widespread among Romans of the upper class. Books were also within reach of less prosperous people because the use of slave labor kept prices relatively low. As many as thirty copies of a work might be made simultaneously by a reader dictating to slave copyists.

The Codex

For four hundred years the roll and the codex existed side by side. There were references to the codex book as early as the first century B.C. By the fourth century A.D., vellum or parchment as a writing material and the codex as a form became dominant, although there are later examples of rolls, and papyrus was occasionally used for official documents until the tenth century.

The substitution of the codex ("manuscript volume, especially of a classic work or of the Scriptures"—*The American Heritage Dictionary of the English Language,* 1969) for the roll was a revolutionary change in the form of the book. The codex is the modern form of the book. Instead of having leaves fastened together on alternate edges to extend in a long strip the codex was constructed from folded leaves bound together on one side—either the right or the left, depending on the direction of the writing.

The codex had several advantages over the roll. A compact pile of pages could be opened instantly to any point in the text, eliminating the cumbersome unrolling and rerolling, and could facilitate the binding of many more leaves in a single book. In addition, the codex made feasible writing on both sides of the leaf; this was not practical for the roll. Because of its compactness, its ease of opening and its use of both sides of the leaf, the codex could conveniently contain longer texts.

It was after Christianity had swept the Roman empire that the codex achieved its supremacy. There was strong motivation for the Christians to preserve the ancient Judaic writings, and the New Testament scriptures; they found the use of the codex and vellum most durable. The most numerous survivals of the early centuries A.D. are the New Testament codices.

With the dissolution of the western Roman empire during the fifth century A.D., and the resultant dominance of marauding barbarians, the very existence of books was threatened. However, books found refuge in monasteries, and the sixth century Rule of St. Benedict enjoined monasteries with the responsibility for making books and creating libraries.

The medieval book was a codex written on vellum or parchment, although by the fifteenth century paper manuscripts became commonplace. Written in a neat book hand that developed into the models from which printing types were drawn, the manscript books of the Middle Ages, in all essential respects, resembled very closely the printed books of the modern period.

The fifteenth century brought the manuscript book to a point where it merged naturally, if perceptibly, into a world of print. In the wake of the humanists, the content of books was enlarged to embrace as large a sphere of human activity as had interested those of classical Greece and Rome. New writers emerged to put books in the language of the people. Literacy was widening. Books were recognized as objects in trade and were handled by guilds as were other articles of commerce. Paper was replacing vellum as the material for books. Creation of the printing press was the next giant step.

Printing

Notwithstanding the popular notion that Johann Gutenberg of Mainz, Germany invented the printing of books on a printing press with movable metal type, it is *not* certain he was originator of this revolutionary development. Though it is known that Gutenberg was experimenting with the process as early as 1439 there is no extant piece of printing which has satisfied the majority of critics that it was definitely done by him. As a matter of fact, the 42-line 1456 Bible known as Gutenberg's is thought by a preponderance of bibliographers to have instead been printed by Johann Fust and Peter Schoffer. Moreover, there are some who believe the Constance missal antidated this renowned 1456 Bible. Though it cannot be said with certainty who was responsible for this extraordinary invention, it can be said that Gutenberg, Fust and Schoffer collectively, are all deserving of recognition and of man's admiration.

Books printed from movable type before 1501 are called *incunabula*. The first dated European book was the Mainz psalter printed by Fust and Schoffer in 1457. So rapid was the spread of printing that by 1500 a press was at work in every major western European country. In a period of a scant 50 years following the invention of printing by mechanical means, more copies of books were made than had been copied the preceding three hundred years.

The distribution of subjects treated by incunabula was as follows: religion 45%, literature 30%, law 10%, science 10%, miscellaneous 5%. As compared with medieval books, incunabula had a high proportion of literature, indicating the influence of the humanist and the vernacular writer.

"Modern" printing techniques so reduced the cost of books that records of the port of London by 1550 show that grocers were importing books for sale along with their more usual merchandise.

The Twentieth Century Book

Numerous intermediate improvements in the techniques of printing, reproduction of illustrations, and materials used took place during the years of printing growth from the fifteenth century development of movable type to the twentieth century book as we know it. Obviously the growth and development of printing and the widespread distribution and use of the book has been due to its peculiar capacity as an instrument of communication. The printed word endures, and the reader can look at it time and again at his own convenience. Thus it is uniquely valuable for the serious student who needs to refresh his memory while laboring through a difficult passage, as well as for transmitting the cultural heritage from one generation to another. In addition, the book is an individual instrument of communication. Silent reading is a solitary act; the reading may go as fast or as slowly as one pleases. Furthermore, the book is relatively cheap to produce. Finally, the book is a compact instrument of communication.

The twentieth century book has been affected by the growth of radio, motion pictures, television and all other media associated with our "Electric Age" as Marshall McLuhan so lucidly describes it. Studies of listening, viewing and reading habits have revealed that more people watch television or listen to the radio than read newspapers; as many view the movies as read magazines; and that a smaller number of people read books as separately published literary products. Yet the newer media have not replaced books. More books are being published and the circulation of magazines and newspapers is higher today than ever before.

One of the important twentieth century developments in book production was the economical photographic process of printing (*lithography*) based on the invention of the photo-offset press in 1904. By this process small numbers of copies, limited editions, can be printed economically as well as larger editions.

The ease with which photographic reproductions of texts can be reduced in size has led to the development of *microtexts*. With a microtext the page of a book may be reduced to as little as 1/200th of its original size, so that it must be read with the aid of a magnifying reader. The obvious advantage of microtext is reduction of bulk in libraries.

The "*microbook*" is part of a system, designed from the user's standpoint, that combines a very high reduction microfiche (a sheet of microfilm) with high resolution readers. The system, recently developed by Encyclopedia Britannica, requires minimal storage space and offers maximum book-reading comfort. The system uses 55 X 90 reductions which make it possible to put 1,000 pages on a single 3 X 5 inch fiche or card. It provides the advantage of unitization— one fiche one book for most single volume works. High resolution readers project microbook images with high quality. A newly developed lap reader from Britannica makes it possible to read books in comfort over extended periods without eye strain.

Book Clubs are another twentieth century innovation in which distributions of huge editions by mail are made at reduced prices to club members. The Book-of-the-Month Club, beginning in 1926, was the first such systematized book distributing organization. Like others of its kind this subscription organization advertises judicious selections heavily, offering book premiums, and reducing prices in accord with its high sales.

The publishing and distribution of *paperbacks* is another twentieth century development which, according to *Saturday Review,* in 1970 produced 15,000 paperback titles by 200 U.S. and 50 Great Britain paper-bound publishers resulting in an annual sale exceeding 300 million copies.

In the same 1971 issue of *Saturday Review* it was reported that *comic books* had reached sales at the phenomenal rate of 40 million copies a month! Beginning with the first comic book, *Famous Funnies,* in 1934 there now are 400 titles on the newstands. Some people denounce the content of comic books as harmful and contributing to juvenile delinquency. Other scholars defend the comic book technique and praise it for introducing children to reading. Surveys indicate that 90 percent of children from ages 7 to 17 have comic books available ranging in types from crime and horror comics to literary classics.

The publication of beautifully illustrated—often in color—*children's books* has become a major business in the twentieth century. This has made possible significant growth over the past seven decades of specialized children's libraries.

One of the developments of the last half of the twentieth century significant to education and libraries is the publication of *programmed texts.* There are a number of variations of programming—e.g. linear, branching, scrambled and modified scramble. It is likely that many future text books will be in some form of programmed learning format. Programmed learning meets nearly all the conditions known to maximize learning. Of course fiction (and other books read for entertainment only) will continue to remain in a format very much as they are today—but where the reading to be done is to acquire utilitarian knowledge, a programmed learning format may become the rule rather than the exception. This will of course have its effect upon the role of the library media center in education.

Reading Habits

How much does twentieth-century man read? Modern statistical reporting yields a fairly clear picture of *habitual* book readers. These statistics reveal the following:

Great Britain	—55%
Australia, Canada, West Germany and the Scandinavian countries	—30 to 45%
United States	—20%

Though American adults are not book readers, they do read. Surveys over a period of 20 years reveal that 60 percent of the adults in the United States read at least one magazine regularly and 85 percent read one or more newspapers daily.

Libraries

A library (from Latin *liber,* "book") by traditional definition is a repository for literary and artistic materials, such as books, periodicals, newspapers, pamphlets, and prints, kept for reading or reference. This definition will be more fully developed and expanded later; however, let us now consider briefly the beginnings and development of libraries.

One thread which has bound the heritage of knowledge throughout all of civilization has been the written word. Libraries—storehouses of recorded knowledge—have existed since earliest history. The conqueror kings of Assyria (ninth to seventh century B.C.) gathered in their capital city of Ninevah a collection (or library) of thousands of clay tablets of cuneiform writing.

However, the first known important institutional libraries came to Athens in the fourth century B.C. with the great schools of philosophy. Aristotle (384-322 B.C.), a philosopher of nearly universal interests, was the first known *systematic* collector of books and as such is deserving of the title "First Librarian" according to Sir F. G. Kenyon in *Books and Readers in Ancient Greece and Rome.*

Schools with libraries took shape in Athens beginning in the third century B.C., and similar institutions (such as the research institute of the Alexandrian museum and Library) began to appear in cities of the eastern Mediterranean shortly thereafter. This great museum-library was organized as an "international" library into faculties, with a president-priest at the head, and the salaries of the staff paid by the king. It is not known how far the ideal of an international library, incorporating not only all Greek literature but also translations into Greek from other languages of the Mediterranean, the Middle-East and India, was realized. According to E. A. Parsons in *The Alexandrian Library: Glory of the Hellenic World,* for the first time the problems of organizing a really large collection, perhaps half a million or more volumes, were faced and the administrators had the vision to see that two preliminary steps were needed: (1) the compilation of a comprehensive bibliography of Greek literature; and (2) the texts that had been acquired, which were probably in a confused state, needed editing and copying in a standard form suitable for easy reference and for storage on a large scale. The rolls and volumes were catalogued into 120 classifications. The great Alexandria Museum and Library survived for six hundred years.

Roman Libraries

The history of Roman libraries for all practical purposes does not begin until 86 B.C. when Sulla brought the Aristotelian collection from Greece and Lucullus brought another great collection from the east in 68 B.C. to form the basis of the famous library at his villa at Tusculum. The most striking feature of Roman libraries was perhaps the spread of private villa collections. From Cicero's time onward the possession of a private library became a necessity to every scholar, teacher, writer and man of affairs. Some of these libraries were surprisingly large; in the third century A.D., one of 62,000 volumes is reported.

In the second century A.D., the establishment of schools at both large and small towns was encouraged and often were subsidized from imperial funds. Libraries followed schools, and there is reason to believe that most cities of the Roman empire possessed municipal libraries where books could be borrowed by the citizenry. By the fourth century A.D. there were twenty-eight public libraries in Rome.

Christian Libraries

Christianity has always been distinguished as a bookish religion, and it was closely associated with the important change in book production that occurred in the first and second centuries A.D., when the roll was being gradually replaced by the modern book or codex. The two most notable early Christian libraries, founded in the sixth century A.D. were one in the community of Vivarium, in southern Italy, founded by Cassidorus, and second, that of the Abbey of Monte Cassino, founded by St. Benedict. Together, these set the pattern for schools, scriptoria (rooms in monasteries set aside for the copying, writing, or adorning of manuscripts and records), and libraries of later monasticism in the west. None of the monastic libraries of the Middle Ages or the Renaissance were large by modern standards; most possessed not more than a few hundred volumes.

The Flowering of Libraries

With the advent of movable-type printing in Germany, more and important libraries began to come into being. Great private, royal, national and university libraries appeared. The Vatican library founded in the fifteenth century, under the first Vatican librarian Bartolomeo Platina, grew to impressive (for that era) size. The Gottingen University library in Germany was the most notable academic library in the eighteenth century. The nineteenth century saw the systematic organization of libraries to meet the rigorous demands of scholarly reference work.

The eighteenth century was particularly notable for the gradual extension of literacy and the habit of reading among all but the humblest classes throughout Europe. Increased literacy led to the development of the popular commercial circulating libraries in the latter half of the eighteenth century. By 1850, literacy was so widespread in England that the first Public Libraries Act was enacted.

The first "public" or institutional library actually to come into existence in the United States was that of Harvard College, when John Harvard left his collection of 260 volumes to the new college in Cambridge in 1638. The first subscription library in the American Colonies was founded by Benjamin Franklin in 1731.

According to 1970 statistics from the U.S. Office of Education, there were about 7000 public libraries, 1500 college and university libraries, 1200 two-year college libraries, 3500 special libraries, 450 law libraries, 800 medical libraries, 475 armed forces and 125 institutional libraries in the United States. Added to these would be approximately 50,000 elementary and secondary school libraries.

The largest library in the United States is the Library of Congress, established in 1800 by Congress. Its extensive collections totalling about 45,000,000 items in 1970 are universal in scope. The New York Public Library, with 7,894,022 volumes in 1967, is the largest public library in the United States. The growth of libraries attached to colleges and universities in the United States has been phenomenal, and some of the university libraries are among the largest in the country. Those with more than 3,000,000 volumes include Harvard University (7,300,000+); University of California (6,300,000+); Yale University (4,800,000+); University of Illinois (3,800,000+); Columbia University (3,500,000+); University of Michigan (3,300,000+).

Among the many names of importance in the history of American library-mediaship are Melvil Dewey, "Father of American Libraries," F. Dean McCluskey, "Father of American Audio-Visual Education," and Andrew Carnegie, "Father of Library Philanthropists."

In Canada, the largest public library is that of Toronto which has more than 1,000,000 volumes. Large Canadian university libraries include those at Toronto, McGill, Queens, and Laval. There are more than 1,500 libraries in Canada.

The oldest national libraries in South America are those of Argentina and Brazil, each founded in 1810; the former has about 300,000 volumes, the later 1,000,000.

Among the great libraries of the world the British Museum with more than 6,000,000 volumes and 60,000 manuscripts remains first in rank. It contains such outstanding treasures as the *Codex Alexandrinus* and the *Codex Sinaiticus* of the Bible, the best collection anywhere of Greek papyri from Egypt, and vast collections of original historical manuscripts of incalculable value.

Other great European libraries include the Bibliothèque Nationale in Paris, France with more than 6,000,000 printed works; the State Library in Berlin, Germany founded in 1659, amalgamated with the University of Berlin in 1947, and serving as a repository for more than 1,500,000 volumes; the Nationolbibliothek in Vienna, Austria with over 1,500,000 volumes, including a fine collection of papyri, theater and motion picture memorabilia; the Biblioteca Nazionale Centrale in Florence, Italy with 4,000,000 volumes. The Lenin State Library in Moscow is reputed to contain 15,000,000 volumes including periodicals; the Leningrad Public Library claims 10,000,000 volumes, and the Library of the Academy of Sciences some 8,000,000 volumes. There are said to be 382,000 libraries in the U.S.S.R. with a total of 1,890,000,000 volumes.

In the Far East, according to the 1970 edition of *Information Please Almanac,* the most extensive libraries are found in Japan. The National Diet Library with its various branches contains an estimated 4,100,000 volumes. The University Library at Kyoto has about 1,820,000. It should, however, be noted that the National Library in Peking, China holds an estimated 4,400,000 volumes.

Media Centers

Media centers go by a number of names. They can and are called just that. They are also called Learning Resources Centers. They are called Learning Centers—and they are *even* called libraries. What distinguishes a media center from the traditional library is its integrated multi-media aspects, its nonprint materials as well as its print materials, its unified materials approach.

Media centers are logical offshoots of the "Electric Age." With the ready availability of power at minimal cost and maximum convenience, a host of audio-visual devices have been developed. Flat pictures, models and the like were in existence in the pre-electric age, but it was electricity that gave birth to radio, motion pictures and television. It was electricity that made it possible to have tape recorders and video-tape recorders. It was electricity that made possible computers, dial-access systems and wet-carrels (study booths wired to accept electrical devices-slide projectors and the like).

The existence of these media marvels has resulted in the capability to rapidly transmit information, to compress the world, to facilitate learning and insofar as libraries are concerned to establish the "Generic Book" (all information in any form).

The modern library or media center utilizes all information sources in media packages to provide the opportunity to optimize learning. Not only do the new library-media centers act as a place where books are kept for use, but through such organizations as the Library-College movement, the thrust is to *take learning to the student*, to individualize learning, to use all of man's communication possibilities, and to have the media center serve as the action-oriented interdisciplinary crossroads of the campus.

Indicative of the dramatic developments taking place in the information sciences during the last third of the twentieth century was the establishment in 1970, under the U.S. Office of Education, of a new *Bureau of Libraries and Educational Technology.* The bureau is responsible for relevant planning functions, coordination of present efforts in the field, technical assistance to projects, and liason with various individuals and organizations working on educational technology.

With the kind of interest being shown in educational communications systems in the United States and elsewhere, the technology now available, and to become available, library-media technologists are bound to be in the exciting-challenging-guiding forefront of the information explosion now upon us.

Prospects and Challenges

The Dallas Public Library System in retrospect is likely to prove to be the embryonic example of library-media services for the future. There, consistent with other forms of "open education" and the stress on other "alternative learning" paths, a learner need not ever attend a class

on a college campus to earn an A.A. degree. His education takes place
entirely inside the Dallas libraries. The library system provides the media
resources, the librarians serve as the learning managers or facilitators.

Additionally, there is study already underway using community libraries
as the primary educational center for acquiring the B.A. degree. Almost
all proposed college and university external degree programs stress the
importance of the central role that the library is to serve in their plans.

What we are seeing in the developed countries of the world is an increasingly sharp educational demand on community resources of all
kinds, but especially on the community libraries. Yet, most community
library systems are ill equipped with respect to nonprint media, wet
carrels, and other learning hardware. Due to library consortia, interloan
services provide the learner with most print needs within a reasonable
length of time. Still, as the public library becomes increasingly transformed into a true learning center more print as well as nonprint resources will be required. Undoubtedly, this will require more financial
aid, aid which is hard to come by.

Just as the *Serrano v. Priest* (California, 1971) decision nullified local
property taxes as the prime source of financial aid to support local schools
it might be expected in the years ahead, as the local public library has increased demands placed upon it, that it, too, may expect greater state
and federal aid. But the inexorable demands of the present require a
sharp shift in the thinking of the past to the realities of the future. The
public library serves largely as a recreational reading center today. Tomorrow it very well may prove to be a community's *chief* learning center.
A look backward will serve as a solid foundation for the now that demands a look ahead to the coming realities.

School and academic libraries, as well as community libraries, are
destined to play an even greater learning role as education increasingly
comes outside the classroom and moves inside the library-media center.
New training as well as new shifts in acquisition policies will be required.
So will new funding sources be required as a new Hellenic Age emerges.

Subsequent chapters will discuss in depth some of the "why" and the
"means" for transforming today's libraries into tomorrow's learning
centers.

LEARNING AND LIBRARY-MEDIA TECHNOLOGY

The design of learning, is either to render a Man an agreeable companion to himself, and teach him to support solitude with pleasure; or, if he is not born to an Estate, to supply that defect, and furnish him with the means of getting one—Anon.

This chapter will introduce the reader to certain research results on student learning which have practical application to both the practicing and future library-media technologist, as well as to various types of media available.

According to *The American Heritage Dictionary of the English Language* a *library* is defined as "a repository for literary and artistic materials, such as books, periodicals, newspapers, pamphlets, and prints, kept for reading or reference." *Media* is defined as "a means of mass communication, such as newspapers, magazines or television." One of the definitions of *technology* is "The application of science . . . using the entire body of methods and materials . . . to achieve objectives." The objective as far as we are concerned is learning.

The definition of a library, of and in itself, suggests a static place—not a place which suggests the excitement that is true of increasing numbers of dynamic libraries sprouting up across the land. Likewise media, of and in itself, does not suggest that the library is the place from which multimedia increasingly radiates. Finally, in our definition, technology standing alone without an objective, has no meaning.

Library Technology

Library technology in the past (and in too many places still) has been concerned *only* with printed material. This is not surprising, for writing has existed for more than 5,000 years in relatively transportable form. Contrast this ancient history with the telegraph, the telephone, the radio, television, computers and other electronic marvels of mass communication which have been in existence for less than a hundred years!

Printed materials still, perhaps without exception, in both public and school libraries, as well as classrooms across the land, remain the *prime* medium of expressing knowledge. This is likely to remain true until at least the turn of the century. Printed material has much to commend itself. It is easily portable. It can be set down and taken up again at a time convenient to the learner. The knowledge presented can be absorbed at varying rates according to the individual ability of each reader. It can't "break-down." It is relatively inexpensive. It allows for reflection.

Much printed material, however, has a new look, particularly in the school setting. Just as there are newer ways of presenting knowledge using nonprint materials, there now are newer ways of presenting printed materials. Though not all *programmed instruction* (PI) is printed, by far the majority of such programs are. PI is a type of educational material for *self-instruction,* as well as a teaching technique. "Automated instruction" and "programmed learning" are terms used synonymously, both with each other, and with "programmed instruction." The common purpose of all PI is to guide the learner so that a particular set of desired changes occur in his performance.

Thus not only has the format of some book and periodical material changed in recent years, thereby raising questions for the library technologist, but the methods available to librarians for cataloging, retrieval of reference information, and circulation controls are also being changed by the increased mechanization available. There are these and other distinct aspects of library technology which the technologist needs to consider. He must take into consideration new developments in book presentation and the purpose of libraries in today's world.

How can the knowledge contained in books, periodicals, pamphlets and other printed materials be most effectively disseminated so as to optimize learning? Is there a difference between what librarians in elementary schools, secondary schools, two-year colleges, four-year colleges, universities, public libraries, and special libraries do? If so, what are the disparate characteristics of these varying institutional types—and what commonalities are shared?

These and similar questions will be taken up in greater depth in subsequent chapters. However, it should be stressed here that the library technologist will largely be successful to the degree that he can motivate and educate *faculty* to *use* his services. This dictum is as nearly true of public librarians as it is of school librarians. Research conducted by the author in 1966 pointed out that "all an instructor had to do, if he wished to have his students use the library extensively, was to assign a term paper, some other written work, or perhaps a speech."

It was further reported that unless an instructor *required* his students to write a term paper, some other written work, or perhaps a speech that the library served little use beyond a quiet place to study *out of textbooks*.

Unless the library technologist can reach faculty who have students accountable to them, the library will remain little more than a collection of books.

To reach the clientele library technologists wish to reach, be they students or adults, requires the skillful employment of communications, persuasion, education and competent service. In short, the library technologist needs to possess the training, qualifications and personal characteristics necessary to effectively compete with the external media of advertising and television.

Media Technology

Media technology has historically been thought of as being restricted to such special communication devices and procedures as radio, cassettes and tapes, recordings, motion pictures, filmstrips, television, graphic illustrations, models, and demonstrations.

As audio-visual devices became readily available they were used increasingly in the educational process largely because as the process of effective learning was analyzed, it became evident that the greater the number of senses which could be engaged in a directed learning activity, the greater would be the learning results, and retention. We now know that learning is still further enhanced when we acknowledge and make use of the affective domain (the emotions and feelings whereby knowledge is acquired) as well as the cognitive domain. In short, the more of the five senses (hearing, seeing, tasting, touching, smelling) we can cause the learner to use, and the more we can emotionally and intellectually involve him in the learning process, the greater the likelihood of his achieving learning mastery.

Just as books, newspapers, pamphlets and periodicals have long proven their worth as powerful transmitters of knowledge, so has research revealed the great effectiveness of nonprint communication devices and means.

Radio and Recordings

Relatively few basic studies have been made to determine the effectiveness of radio and recordings in teaching factual information and in changing attitudes and interests. However, it seems to the author that radio and recordings are at least as effective as conventional teaching methods, and they are liked by students.

Mixed research results favoring radio over conventional classroom procedures have been reported with respect to current events. Haugh (1952) on the one hand found no significant differences in the effectiveness of reading or listening to the radio in acquiring information or shifting attitudes. On the other hand, Rothney and Hansen (1947) report greater effectiveness of radio for the acquisition of information and for shifting student attitudes. In other findings Lowdermilk (1939) found that reading was more effective than listening in influencing students' attitudes toward freedom of speech and assembly, but that reading the script of the recording while listening was more effective than reading alone. Rulon (1944) found recordings of little value in motivating students to further study. Reid (1940) found that a series of broadcasts failed to stimulate seventh and eighth grade students' interest in reading.

It is not surprising that radio has proven less effective a means of transmitting knowledge than instructional films and television. In the case of radio essentially only one sense (hearing) is involved in the learning process whereas with instructional films and television two of the five senses are engaged in the learning process—hearing and seeing.

Filmstrip, Slides and Single-Concept Loop Films

Since *filmstrips, slides* and *single-concept loop films* are among the most economical of AV materials their effectiveness as compared with more expensive instructional films and television has frequently been studied.

Early studies by McClusky (1924) et al comparing filmstrips and slides with the *silent* motion picture found in general that the projected still pictures were about as effective in teaching factual information as silent films.

Later studies once again comparing filmstrips and slides with *sound* motion pictures have supported those earlier findings. Carson (1947) reported a study made by the Scottish Educational Film Association in which long and abbreviated versions of a filmstrip on American cowboys were compared with a sound film on the same subject. As measured by a 40-item true-false and multiple-choice test, the two filmstrip groups were greatly superior to the sound film groups in learning information and concepts. Heidgerken (1948), on the other hand, found no differences among filmstrips, instructional films, and filmstrips combined with instructional films in teaching units in a course on nursing arts. Houland and others (1949) compared the effectiveness of an Army training film on map reading with an Army filmstrip that presented the same content and found that Army Quartermaster trainees, tested by a 39-item verbal and visualized test, learned slightly, but not statistically significantly more, from the filmstrip.

Jackson (1948) found filmstrips made from frames of motion pictures on the life of St. Paul to have about the same teaching value as the film itself in teaching the Bible to high-school students. Abramson (1952) studied the relative effectiveness of two methods of teaching a year course in elementary mechanics to students in a large city high school where various socio-economic factors produced a general lack of interest in school work. He studied the value of the standard method of instruction (which combined recitation, demonstration, film, supervised study, and laboratory exercises) with a method using the projection of pictorial ideograms (a character or symbol representing an idea or thing without expressing a particular word or phrase for it, as the characters in Chinese) as slides, each slide followed by several "thought" questions which focused on certain elements and relationships in the slides. Achievement was measured by specially prepared tests given immediately and two months later. The slide group achieved significantly more learning than the control group on all three units of instruction on both the immediate and the two-month retention tests. Kale and Grosslight (1955) studied the learning of Russian vocabulary under several conditions, including pictures plus titles *versus* titles only, motion *versus* still pictures, and sound *versus* silent pictures. They found: (1) pictures of an object or act were an aid to learning vocabulary; (2) still pictures were as effective as motion pictures; (3) pronunciation of the words by a narrator seemed to *inhibit* learning to write the words.

Butts (1956) studied the comparative effectiveness of captions on slides. He found that declarative and imperative captions were significantly superior to interrogative captions in helping students learn and retain information.

Multi-media presentations which present two or more pictures on several screens simultaneously with synchronized commentary have recently become popular. These impressive multisensory presentations though may not be the reason for the increased learning that a few studies have demonstrated. The careful organization and presentation of instructional content may make the greatest contribution to increased learning.

Pictorial Illustrations

Although there has been little research on the *effectiveness* of pictorial illustration or "flat" pictures, picture *preference* studies (Knowlton et al) reveal that children prefer illustrations that (1) are colored; (2) contain action; (3) tell a story; (4) are related to previous experiences and can be associated with places, objects, persons, events, or animals about which they have read or with which they are familiar; (5) are large in size.

Educational Films

Extensive research has been conducted in the use of films in education. Research evidence clearly supports the evidence that films can teach factual information effectively over a wide range of subject-matter content, ages, abilities and conditions of use. Meierhenry (1952, 1955) reported that Nebraska high school classes, devoting one-sixth of their instructional time in certain course areas to the use of educational films, made significantly better scores than nonfilm classes on informational tests directly related to the content of the films, and equal scores on standardized tests. Wise (1949) found film groups superior to nonfilm groups in teaching high-school biology.

VanderMoor (1950) found that a body of factual information such as general science could be taught by films alone almost as effectively as by a teacher using conventional classroom procedures and even better if the films were introduced or supplemented by brief study guides.

Research results have also established that educational films effectively teach such perceptual motor skills as improved handwriting and athletic proficiencies. Films also are superior to traditional teaching methods in teaching complex occupationally oriented skills.

Instructional films have been subject to frequent criticism by critics who assert that such learning is "passive" and therefore interferes with thinking and the development of concepts and inferences. The evidence, however, is on the side of the film in developing concepts as revealed by research conducted by Rulon (1933) and Vernon (1946). Furthermore as long ago as 1929; Knowlton and Tilton found in their research studies that the use of films increased classroom participation and voluntary reading.

There is no evidence that film is superior to other communication media in influencing *general* attitudes. In fact, research has shown little evidence that films change general attitudes *if* they are contrary to the existing beliefs, personality structure, or the social-cultural environment of the individual viewing the film presentation. Indeed, if the film attempts to promote an attitude in direct conflict with an individual's personal attitude or a social norm, it is likely to result in negative reinforcement, i.e., reinforcing the existing attitude rather than changing it. On the other hand, it also appears that the cumulative effect of a *series* of films on the same theme, can create lasting attitudinal changes if the attitudinal theme stressed is not completely in opposition to existing beliefs.

Television

Like instructional films, television has also been found to be efficacious. Research has consistently revealed that teaching by television is effective at all levels of instruction and in all types of situations. Instructional television has been found to be inferior to conventional instruction in only a few cases, and in many cases TV was found to be significantly more effective. What is now considered to be the classical study of instructional television was Brish's 1964 report on the elementary schools of Hagerstown, Maryland. With a budget of $280,000 a year students in grades 1-6 were able to spend 10 percent of their classroom time utilizing television, while junior high school students spent almost one-third of their time in television classes. Student achievement improved significantly and it was possible to upgrade the curriculum and enrich the educational programs more readily and economically.

The considerable number of studies made with respect to learning by instructional television on college campuses reveals that television is equal to, or superior to, conventional instruction in such courses as general chemistry, general psychology, psychology of marriage, business law, elementary biology, typewriting and others. Moreover, it has been found that the learning of subject matter is *not* adversely affected by assignment to large TV sections over smaller ones (Macomber, 1956; Driscoll, 1957, Schram, 1969).

Television has also proved its value in teaching adult students viewing

TV from their homes; as a matter of fact, such students earn *higher* grades than regular campus students. However, it should be borne in mind that the TV student is older on the average, is likely to be enrolled in but one or two courses, and is probably more highly motivated than his younger full-time counterpart on campus. Notwithstanding these factors, such results clearly demonstrate the power of the medium for imparting knowledge. However, it should be borne in mind that Kanner, Kosenstein (1960) and others have demonstrated that color television is no better than black-and-white television in furthering cognitive learning.

Student Reaction to Instructional Television has resulted in mixed reactions. Fritz (1952) and others have reported a positive bias by students toward instructional television. On the other hand, Carpenter and Greenhill (1955), as well as others, have reported a negative bias by students toward courses taught by television. However, it has been found that those students holding a negative bias toward television instruction can and do overcome this negative attitude when they perceive their television instructor as to be of "excellent" quality. In short, studies have shown that students overwhelmingly will enroll in a TV or large class section *if* assured that their instructor is of known excellence.

Video Tape Recorders (VTR)

Video tape recorders are well known by the television industry and viewers. More often than not, television programs are "taped" rather than "live." Taped shows have been "filmed" by video tape cameras at a convenient time to be "played back" later according to a telecast schedule. One of the clearest examples of video tape recording versatility is evident in viewing sporting events. The so-called "instant replay" of a spectacular baseball play or a football touchdown is well known. Like the sound tape recorder, the sound-sight video tape recorder has excellent instructional capabilities. Athletes can immediately view their mistakes. Students in speech classes can immediately review their presentations. Social science simulations (the act or process of imitating the appearance, form or sound of another) such as a reenactment of the impeachment trial of Andrew Johnson in a history class can be effectively reviewed for historical errors in perception and discussion.

If a "world wide" agreement on standardizing VTR tapes can be achieved, and if the strong trend toward packaging VTR tapes in cartridges continues, great promise is in store for VTR. VTR tapes can be readily played through an ordinary television receiver. VTR's strength lies in its capability of recording live classroom and other events as well as TV programs.

VTR Cartridges

VTR *cartridges* likely will, as Marshall McLuhan has suggested, give man "new needs, goals, and desires . . . upset all political, educational and commercial establishments."

Another well known "futurist" also to be heard is Alvin Toffler *(Future Shock)*, who predicts that the cartridge will boost rates of change in every sector of Western culture. The *Saturday Review* says the cartridge means Everyman will soon have "total access to such of the world's wisdom and pleasure as eyes and ears may receive." Jack Gould of *The New York Times* says it means Everyman will soon be free of the domination of the industry's "professionals." ("In the case of a tour of the Louvre, for instance, the TV director would have no choice in how long one might stare at the 'Mona Lisa!' [If the viewer presses the cartridge player's freeze button] the smile could be kept on the screen all night.")

Peter Goldmark, the inventor of the cartridge, says the cartridge is "going to be the greatest revolution in communications since the book." Through the use of "sound, new kinds of printing, three-dimensional printing," it will provide a means of recovering reading from the limbo into which it has fallen among the young. It also provides access to materials hitherto either too expensive or cumbersome to store. The content of the entire *Encyclopedia Britannica* can be stored on a single cartridge, priced under $15, says Benjamin DeMott, ETV consultant. And Goldmark has already perfected an instrument by means of which the viewer can swiftly find the page he wants.

It may be that Goldmark, DeMott and other enthusiasts of VTR cartridges are being seriously carried away in one very important respect. The claims for low cost—ranging from $5 to $150, depending on such factors as color, length, topic, production costs, market, etc.—are likely to prove totally misleading at least with copyrighted materials. For instance, it hardly seems realistic that *Encyclopedia Britannica* will permit their $500 set of volumes to instead be sold for $15 in a cartridge format.

The cartridge does have obvious and powerful educational possibilities. Today students often demand individualized and "customized" curricula adjusted to eccentric individual tastes. A VTR library could provide the poorest college in the nation with a catalog of "course alternatives" comparable to those available at the greatest universities. Enthusiasm for "universities without walls," field study, experimental education, engagement with The Real, grows steadily. With VTR regional centers, an undergraduate might backpack for years without ever missing a "class," taking his degree (if degrees are still given in the future) through a single set of final exams at the time of his choice. (The English educational system already allows variation in degree examination scheduling.) Conceivably, VTR libraries could free teachers for the kind of intensive "Mark Hopkins on a log" tutorials necessary for the less well-prepared students. And, too, both the academic and community library is destined to play an increasingly important role as education increasingly becomes "deschooled" and hence less formalized.

Practitioners in medicine and other professions hunger for practical ideas of continuing education, ways of keeping in touch with advances in their field. The use of cartridges, either through contracts between professional societies and individual practitioners or library-media centers could guarantee life-time, at-home access to the best that's known and done, year by year, in one's profession.

Table 1 below is indicative of the multi-varied packaged video-sound systems now on the market. There is no question that the would-be library-media technologist will need to keep up-to-date on newer developments as they emerge. These developments will soon have profound effects on the teaching-learning process and what the Library-Media Center is to *become.*

Three-Dimensional Materials

Most of the research on the values of three-dimensional materials has been done by the Armed Services, and business and industry rather than by schools.

There has been, however, some study of the effectiveness of three dimensional materials. Uris (1955), after finding that complex motor skills such as threading a motion-picture projector could be taught better by three-dimensional models than by two-dimensional aids, concluded that 3-D materials should be used where the task to be learned is essentially three-dimensional in nature.

The most exciting and promising 3-D development to have emerged during the past decade unquestionably has been *holography.* Emerging from the practical outcomes of research in laser [L(ight) A(mplification by) S(timulated) E(mission of) R(adiation)] beam technology a radical

Table 1
Characteristics, Aspects, and Features of Packaged Video Systems

System Developer Manufacturer	Introduced	Medium	Player Only	Combined Player-Recorder	Est Cost When Integral Unit In Larger System ($)	Est Cost As Self-contained Unit ($)	Least Favorable Material Cost Per Minute ($)	Maximum Uninterrupted Player–Record Time (minutes)	Inter-Manufacturer Agreed Upon Standard
AEG Telefunken (Teledec Videodisc)	1972	Disc	X				0.05	12	
Ampex Corporation (Instavision)	Mid 1971	Magnetic		X		8–1,000	0.43	60	EIA-J Type 1–b&w
Cartridge Television Inc. (Cartrivision)	Early 1971	Magnetic		X	8–900	4–500	0.66	120	EIA-J Type 1–b&w
Nord Mende (Germany)	1972	Photo-graphic	X			560	2.13 cir 1.20 b&w	30	Super 8 mm

new way to project visual images has been achieved. The holograph was
first developed as a laboratory technique to reduce the spherical aberra-
tion in high-magnification electron microscopes. However, as a result of a
number of imaginative experiments, holography has now been developed
to the point where spectacular esthetic effects and images have been projected in a way never before possible.

The hologram, in essence, is a true three-dimensional pictorial representation of a given object, made by exposing a special photographic film plate
to laser light that has been reflected from the real object. When this negative or slide is projected by the same laser beam that created it, it presents
an image possessing almost all the physical qualities of the object and, perhaps most important, accurate perspective views of the sides, top, and
bottom.

The word "hologram" comes from the Greek "holos" which means
whole or complete, the entire record. For study purposes the holographic
image is the next best thing to having the actual object present. Its ability
to reproduce objects in 3-D without the need of any optical devices by
the viewer makes holography potentially among the most promising of
all media aids.

The hologram now makes accessible to the instructor and his students
the whole universe of three-dimensional objects in a manner never before
possible. Equally important is the fact that the holographic slide does not
take up much more room than an ordinary 35 mm slide now widely used
for reproducing two-dimensional images. The basic components of a
simple laser holography system can be set up and made operational for a
relatively modest expenditure.

Though the laser was developed as recently as 1960, it already is anticipated that this remarkable invention will before long be used to project
TV images in theaters and in homes, to print books, to create book-sized
electronic computers and to become the primary means for transmitting
radio and television signals throughout the world. If all this does happen,
it will undoubtedly cause a decided change in aims and technology of the
library-media center.

There are, of course, a number of other important media devices that
have not been discussed in detail. The *opaque projector* though important
is largely being replaced by the *overhead projector* which can project easily
made transparencies. *Magnetic chalkboards,* rather than *slate chalkboards,*
are on the increase making it possible to inexpensively illustrate three-di-

mensional relationships in such areas as mathematics and science. The availability of *microfilm* and *microfiche* readers in school media centers is becoming increasingly common as is also true in the case of public and specialized libraries. *Dial access systems* are becoming more available. Easily portable light weight *cassette tape recorders and players* are widely used. Even "total" packaged media centers are being manufactured and coming into use.

The foregoing suggests the need for knowledge workers to become familiar with research as related to the relationship between materials and learning since, increasingly, the role of the librarian and educational technologist will be that of teacher and tutor.

Library-media technologists will increasingly be called upon to produce just the right "mix" of learning materials and resources so as to optimize learning. Moreover, as "formal" education increasingly becomes the primary function of the library-media center, not only must the professional knowledge worker "cyberneticize" the learning environment but he must also know what instructional techniques and procedures most facilitate the acquisition of knowledge and skills. The next chapter discusses what is a new role for most of today's library-media technologists.

THE LIBRARY-MEDIA CENTER IN THE
EDUCATIONAL PROCESS

*Knowledge is of two kinds. We know a subject ourselves, or we
know where we can find information upon it*—Samuel Johnson

Just as library technology can no longer be thought of as only consisting of printed materials, likewise media technology can no longer be thought
of as only consisting of nonprint materials. In today's library-media center
all *educational communicatons media* must be merged. Furthermore, the
library-media technologist must be knowledgable concerning the newer
methodologies and techniques in education and be prepared to cooperate
fully in the educational process.

The first function of media is to *supplement* not supplant the teacher
by increasing his effectiveness in the classroom. The second media function utilizes media alone for instruction. Media may thus be used to enrich existing instruction or to improve overall productivity through instructional media systems which do not depend upon the teacher for
routine presentation of instructional material.

The Carnegie Commission on Educational Television (1967) described
the role of television in providing general education to the public through
a nationwide system of public television stations. This is a trend toward
providing education whenever needed rather than confining it to our
schools. For many years correspondence courses have provided instruction using books alone. Now courses of instruction are being taught by
television, programmed texts, filmed courses, radio, tapes, records, teaching machines, electronic classrooms, computer-assisted instruction, and
sound filmstrips. Educational media are often used alone to provide instruction. However, the major use of communications media is to supplement the teacher by enhancing his effectiveness in the classroom.

The teacher today can call upon a myriad of instructional materials for
assistance in the teaching-learning process. About 5,000 new films, filmstrips, tapes, recordings, models, and graphic materials become available
each year. *The Educational Media Index,* prepared under the direction of

the Educational Media Council, consists of 14 volumes and lists almost 30,000 items. A particularly valuable film which can be used effectively in conjunction with this particular chapter is *Resources for Learning* (Educational Media Book Co.).

Not only does instruction utilizing educational communications media prove to be generally effective, but research has shown that such media is capable of assuming a substantial portion of the task of providing information in the classroom, thereby permitting the instructor to become a manager of learning situations, a supervisor of instruction and a counselor of students.

The media specialist and his technicians and aides have as their primary function the responsibility, as members of the instructional team, to further student learning success. To be effective, each member of the instructional team (the library-media personnel as well as faculty and administrator) needs to possess certain common overlapping knowledge as well as specialized knowledge. Thus library-media technologists need some basic knowledge of research results with regard to the principles of learning and their theoretical and philosophical understructures.

Perhaps Marshall McLuhan* better than any modern day philosopher, best expresses the understructures of theory and philosophy as regards to media:

> After three thousand years of explosion, by means of fragmentary and mechanical technologies, the Western world is imploding. During the mechanical ages we had extended our bodies in space. Today, after more than a century of electric technology, we have extended our central nervous system itself in a global embrace, abolishing both space and time as far as our planet is concerned. Rapidly, we approach the final phase of the extension of man—the technological simulation of consciousness, when the creative process of knowing will be collectively and corporately extended to the whole of human society, much as we have already extended our senses and our nerves by the various media.

Probably McLuhan's phrase "The medium is the message" is best known and most clearly identified with him. He aptly explains:

*_____

Understanding Media by Marshall McLuhan. © 1964, McGraw-Hill Book Co., New York. Used with permission of McGraw-Hill Book Company.

In a culture like ours, long accustomed to splitting and dividing all things as a means of control, it is sometimes a bit of a shock to be reminded that, in operational and practical fact, the medium is the message. This is merely to say that the personal and social consequences of any medium—that is, of any extension of ourselves—result from the new scale that is introduced into our affairs by each extension of ourselves, or by any new technology. . . . The instance of the electric light may prove illuminating in this connection. The electric light is pure information. It is a medium without a message, as it were, unless it is used to spell out some verbal ad or name. This fact, characteristic of all media, means that the "content" of any medium is always another medium. The content of writing is speech, just as the written word is the content of print, and print is the content of the telegraph. If it is asked, "What is the content of speech?," it is necessary to say, "It is an actual process of thought, which is in itself nonverbal."

. . . it is only too typical that the "content" of any medium blinds us to the character of the medium. It is only today that industries have become aware of the various kinds of business in which they are engaged. When IBM discovered that it was not in the business of making office equipment or business machines, but that it was in the business of processing information, then it began to navigate with clear vision. . . .The electric light escapes attention as a communication medium just because it has no "content." And this makes it an invaluable instance of how people fail to study media at all. For it is not till the electric light is used to spell out some brand name that it is noticed as a medium. Then it is not the light but the "content" (or what is really another medium) that is noticed. The message of the electric light is like the message of electric power in industry, totally radical, pervasive, and decentralized. For electric light and power are separate from their uses, yet they eliminate time and space factor in human association exactly as do radio, telegraph, telephone, and TV, creating involvement in depth.

Lateral (creative) versus Vertical (logical) Thinking

Edward de Bono, of Cambridge University, England, also helps us view our surroundings by means of *lateral thinking* (1970): i.e., nonlogical, creative thinking. Lateral thinking can best be appreciated when seen in action as the following instance.

The experts laughed at Marconi's idea that he could transmit a signal across the Atlantic. They assured him that since wireless waves traveled in straight lines, they would not follow the curvature of the earth but would fly off into space. Logically, the experts were correct. But Marconi tried, persisted, and succeeded in sending a signal across the Atlantic. Neither he nor the "experts" knew about the ionosphere, which bounced back the wireless waves that would have otherwise streamed off into space as predicted. Had Marconi been rigidly logical all along, he would have abandoned his idea.

Opposed to lateral thinking is *vertical* (logical) *thinking.* Vertical thinking has the great disadvantage of needing to be right each step of the way. That is the very essence of logic. But this need to be right at every stage is probably the biggest bar there is to new ideas. With lateral thinking, only the final conclusion need be correct.

Both McLuhan and de Bono have pointed out the importance of creative thinking as well as logical thinking. Both kinds of thinking are necessary attributes of library-media technologists. To acquire lateral thinking skills may require no more than a shift in emphasis from the obvious way of looking at something to a less obvious way.

Knowledge transmission

In education, probably the conventional method (textbook and lecture/ chalk and talk) is most in need of lateral thinking. It is the role of the library-media technologist to assist faculty to enter the "Electric Age" and to *effectively* use the resultant media available to aid student learning.

Illustrative of the traditional teacher's dependence on the lecture method is a tale, probably apocryphal, of a student taking a lecture class who *was* aware of the Electric Age he was living in though his instructor, obviously, was not. He was struck by the insight that all that was required to pass the course was to "store" information and "retrieve" it at test time. His lecturer permitted him to tape-record the lecture, and the student retired to read in the library. Other students soon were doing the same, until the astonished lecturer realized he was orating to a roomful of machines. So the lecturer taped his lecture at home and had it talk to the student recorders. All then pursued their educations in the library!

One other insightful student in the class was alleged to have remarked that if the lecture were printed, he could read it at 400 to 500 words per minute while the spoken word speed was only at a rate of 130 words per minute. The professor, therefore, had his lectures printed and a new book went into the library.

The lecture form of instruction has been used extensively since the Middle Ages and even before. However, with the advent of swarms of students the lecture has become increasingly monologish as well as more text-parroting. Meanwhile many texts have become more encyclopedic and dull! The student can avoid reading the text by listening carefully and taking good notes—or can avoid attending class sessions except for test taking by carefully reading the text. What is even worse, a poor, un-challenging lecture can actually *inhibit* learning.

The use of programmed instruction and other multi-sensory mediated instruction in which the learner is an *active* participant in the learning process is necessary for effective learning to result. The learner may very well be passive in the sense of physical activity, but passivity of *mental* processes precludes learning. The library-media technologist, working as a full participant on the instructional team, has a major contribution to make to ensure a unified media program in which the instructor, the stu-dents, printed materials and audiovisual media, are all combined together in such a way that learning is optimized. This arrangement is called "cybernation."

Library-media technologists, as learning managers, need to be aware that not only can media be adjunctive to a central role played by a teacher, but at times it is the media which should be central and the teacher who should be adjunctive.

Historically, as audio-visual devices and materials were successfully in-troduced into schools, they were considered adjunctive aids to teachers. They were *not* conceived as self-contained instructional packages, and utilization procedures assumed the necessity of an instructor to complete the instructional task. Although certain research studies and some pro-grams, notably in the armed forces, have proved that audio-visual materials can be far more than "aids," the practice of treating media as aids still largely prevails.

As a matter of fact, experience with the newer technologies of instruc-tion (television, VTRs, holographic film, programmed instruction, language laboratories, CAI, etc.) indicate that they can often be treated as self-contained knowledge transmitting units rather than "aids." Indeed, media specialists, working in conjunction with faculty, can assign major instructional tasks to mediated instruction with confidence. While it is possible to reduce technologies of instruction to aids, it is evident that their *intended* use breaks the traditional instructional pattern. Mediated instruction is not just intended to "extend" the classroom teacher. On the contrary, it can represent effective *alternate* ways of fostering quality education.

Reordering of Instructional Modes

Education which emphasizes quality need not cost more than existing common practices in most schools, colleges and universities. However, quality education does require the adoption of newer policies and procedures utilized today in only a small number of educational institutions, although quite widely accepted by business, industry and military establishments.

What is quality education? Quality education is the successful accomplishment of the maximum amount of demonstrable perceptive, psychomotive and affective knowledge, by individuals with a wide range of abilities, in the minimum amount of time, optimizing the investment of human, physical, equipment and material resources.

In this definition, four specific emphases require attention:

1. Individuals with a wide range of abilities—programs must be developed for all rather than just the extremely able.

2. Successful accomplishment by the individual in demonstrable cognitive and/or psychomotive and/or affective areas must be emphasized.

3. Amount of time consumed in learning must be recognized as one of the most important variables. It varies significantly from individual to individual and even for the same individual with different tasks. Thus the hour, day, week, and certainly the semester have no significance as measures of time for learning, and these must be varied for the individual and the task.

4. The investment of human, physical, equipment and material resources must be strategically utilized for the maximum individual results.

The need to systematize and mediate instructional strategies is clearly evident if we are willing to clearly face the fact that our schools are in need of vast improvements. Even more important is the need for educational practitioners to have the courage to reorder American education by substituting scientific practices for "art" and archaic habits of the past (and present). We *do* have the know-how.

Pointing up the failure of our lecture-text and talk-chalk conventional "art" system of imparting knowledge is the dismal fact that only eight

of 25 million Americans needing vocational training are presently enrolled in such programs. The 1969 report of the National Advisory
Council on Vocational Education (from which the following excerpt is
taken) put the problem well:

> At the very heart of our problem is a national attitude that says
> vocational education is designed for somebody else's children. This
> attitude is shared by businessmen, labor leaders, administrators,
> teachers, parents and students. We are all guilty. We have promoted
> the idea that the only good education is an education capped by
> four years of college. This idea, transmitted by our values, our as-
> pirations and our silent support, is snobbish, undemocratic and a
> revelation of why schools fail so many students.
>   The attitude must change. The number of jobs which the unskilled
> can fill is declining rapidly. The number requiring a liberal arts educa-
> tion, while growing, is increasing far less rapidly than the number de-
> manding technical skill. In the 1980's, it will still be true that fewer
> than 20 percent of our job opportunities will require a four-year
> college degree.
>   In America, every child must be educated to his highest potential,
> and the height of the potential is not measured by the color of the
> collar. Plumbers, carpenters and electricians make more than many
> school superintendents and college presidents; only the arrogant
> will allow themselves to feel that one is more worthy than the other.

John Gardner, former Secretary of the Department of Health, Education and Welfare, forcefully states the kind of attitude that needs to
emerge in America:

> . . . There may be excellent plumbers and incompetent plumbers,
> excellent philosophers and incompetent philosophers. An excellent
> plumber is infinitely more admirable than an incompetent philoso-
> pher. The society which scorns excellence in plumbing because plumb-
> ing is a humble activity and tolerates shoddiness in philosophy because
> it is an exalted activity, will have neither good plumbing nor good
> philosophy. Neither its pipes nor its theories will hold water.*

*From "Quality in Higher Education" by John Gardner in *Current Issues in Higher
Education* 1958 (Washington, D.C.: Association for Higher Education, 1958), p. 15.

Library-media technologists can play a significant role in helping overcome the "color of the collar" syndrome.

Telling students what they will be able to do at the end of a particular unit could well be the single most significant thing an instructor can do to effect learning. In short, probably the most effective way to help a student achieve is to tell him exactly what he will accomplish and then convince him that the instructor is committed to see that requisite learning *does* result.

As a separate educational enterprise, the Army operates what Peter Kim of AMPEX describes as the world's largest campus—the Army School System—comprising two colleges, 22 branch schools and specialist schools, offering 650 courses of instruction in 17 states. Connecting many of these schools, the Army today operates the largest ETV network in the country, if not in the world. The application of modern technology to education and training is not a research toy—it is a fact and way of life. Our schools can tap this rich resource if the interest in doing so is keen enough. The State of Utah has arranged through the *Air Force Association's Aerospace Education Foundation* to have access to non-security classified training programs, courses, lesson plans, and other materials used in the Air Force Training Program. These resources are open to all our schools as a result of the passage of the Public Information Act. These resources should be made use of.

Measurable Learning Outputs

It should now be apparent that objectives are more important than media. The media become part of the system—but are not *the* system. Media and human resources are combined into a cybernetic model designed to achieve carefully programmed behavioral learning outputs. Once an instructor sets objectives, he is virtually forced to find appropriate instructional media. It is here that the library-media technologist plays a particularly crucial role as a member of the instructional team. Students who are learning in a situation in which objectives have been specified and communicated to them *in advance* of the course refuse to tolerate shoddy media and irrelevant and shoddy lecturing. In many instances the library-media technologist, working with the instructor, must retrieve or create the materials necessary to assist the student in achieving learning mastery.

Presented with objectives for the first time, students exhibit intriguing behavior patterns that point up the inadequacies of ambiguous goals. Habituated to the educational guessing game they repeatedly search for the "catch." Finding none they often remark that they were released for *thinking* about the subject matter. Students realize that by communicating exactly what they were to do, the instructor removed a screen, a veil of secrecy, from between himself and them.

Cohen (1969) has suggested that "in many instructional situations, students themselves could very beneficially participate in setting objectives in advance of the course. The actual writing of objectives thus can be part of the learning process. Too, students' acceptance of objectives as being worthy of their attention may be enhanced. As students work with instructors in building specific ends for the course in which they are involved, they learn to focus on the consequences of their actions. That alone is an important activity, one which can be itself a valid goal."

Measurable learning objectives consist of a *task* to be performed, *conditions* under which the task is to be performed, and the *criterion,* or qualitative level, at which the task is to be achieved. Frequently this system is designated as *behavioral objectives* since a change in cognitive and/or affective behavior is supposed to result. The programmed learning format is the *media means* whereby learning mastery of the knowledge presented is facilitated.

To determine if a programmed text meets the conditions to cause learning, to write meaningfully behavioral learning outputs, to evaluate instruction, to determine if libraries (i.e. media centers, learning resource centers, learning centers) are causing learning, we must turn to basic psychological foundations of learning theory. In a hundred years of research into human learning *only* four axioms have proven true:

1. Learning is facilitated if a person *wants to learn* (motivation)

2. Learning is facilitated if a person *knows what he is supposed to learn* (expectations)

3. Learning is facilitated if a person is *actively involved* in the learning exercise (participation)

4. Learning is facilitated if a person has *knowledge of results* (feedback)— *the sooner the better* (reinforcement)

All instructional systems need to incorporate those four axioms. Ancillary to the four axioms are two supportive techniques to facilitate learning: (1) the more of the five senses used in the learning process the greater will be the learning, and (2) learning will be enhanced if the learner or the learner's group is treated in a special way. Anyone engaged in the process of setting learning conditions needs to test his system against these axioms and supportive techniques. Failure to do so, is to defeat the purpose of education and to squander scarce financial resources.

Uses of Media in Instructional Systems

A few concrete illustrations of the use of media in a systems approach will illuminate the multi-varied possibilities which suggest both vertical and lateral thinking.

Education appears to be one of the last frontiers for the technological revolution to change—a revolution that has so drastically changed modern life. Refrigerators and freezers, dishwashers and disposals, and automatic washers and dryers have long since transformed homes. Automobiles and jet propelled planes have radically altered travel. But no such revolution has yet re-made education.

Perhaps a high regard for the personal bond needed between a teacher and his students has led some to be slow in accepting those changes that technology can make in education. Perhaps there is a belief that too much media might sever this teacher-student link. But, as a matter of fact, using media can make teaching *more,* not less, *personal.*

A mother who saves two hours a day with an automatic washer, dryer, and dishwasher can use that time to do more things with her children. By the same token, a teacher who saves time by using media for certain routine matters, drills, or basic presentations of fact can use the saved time for more counseling, more discussion, better evaluation of assignments, and better planning and preparation of presentations.

For example, *tape recording* certain materials on grammar in *English Composition* so that students can work on drills and exercises without requiring time from the teacher frees the teacher to become more of a learning manager. Normally, students will use a workbook while listening to instructional tape recordings. The workbook provides visuals such as charts, maps, or photographs and keeps the student active by asking him to fill in blanks, answer questions, or take notes. Other tapes can present background material on principles of composition and biographical information on certain authors being studied. With the saved time, the teacher can do a more careful job of marking the papers turned in and can still have time for individual conferences with students needing special help. The student is not in the classroom with the teacher as many hours a week, but he has even closer personal contact with him

AUDIO-TUTORIAL INSTRUCTION IN ENGLISH COMPOSITION

Photographed at Mt. San Jacinto College, California by Robert Jamieson.
Photo courtesy of the college.

because of the attention given individually and in small groups during the time saved.

General biology presents another application designed to achieve this same end. Here the teacher can have recorded material to be used with a book of drawings to acquaint students with material they will work with in the laboratory. The teacher saves laboratory time because students know more when they come. The teacher is also freed from the necessity of taking lab time to lecture so students will know what they are to do and how they are to do it. The teacher, then, can "float" from one student to another in the lab, working with each individually.

In the *chemistry* laboratory another mediated technique results in a similar outcome. Single concept films are available on how to use various types of equipment. By having a single concept projector available in the lab, the teacher can let the student plug the cartridge into the projector and by himself see how to use the equipment. Thus, the teacher allows recordings or films to do some things for him so that he can use the time saved for students who need help not available by mediation.

A major problem of nonsystematized education has been that most of the time a teacher must deal with students in groups where all must proceed at about the same speed. By mediating certain materials, however, the teacher can allow greater variations and thus provide more individualization of the process. This individualizing of learning can be accomplished through the "systems" approach or through the "open classroom" approach to learning.

In *Music for Elementary Teachers,* for example, there has always been the problem of students entering the class with a wide disparity of musical background. Should the teacher take class time to bring the weak ones up to where the stronger ones already are, thus wasting the time of many and boring the strong ones in the class? Or, should the teacher devote out-of-class time to special work with those who are weak when his time is already limited? The answer should be "no" to both questions because there is a third choice: By *recording* certain materials in advance (in time provided for this), the teacher can have ready a variety of materials for use. The weaker students can then use these as much as necessary without taking time from either the teacher or from students who do not need the extra material. Thus a student who needs work in rhythm, key signatures, or intervals can study these as long as he needs to without being a drag on the class. He gets individual attention and the class is improved.

Again, in all *shorthand* classes some students move along more rapidly than others. Mediation can make it possible for students who need dictation at various speeds to receive this personalized attention. At Oklahoma Christian, for example, students may dial shorthand dictation at different speeds in their carrels, and there are also ways available to provide this variation even in the classroom.

The *language laboratory* is probably the best known instance of providing for individual needs through mechanization since it allows a student to cover material as needed and as adapted to his level. The teacher cannot do this while working with the entire class, but by mechanization the personalization is made possible.

Another illustration of meeting individual needs by mechanical means comes from *private music lessons.* A voice teacher can record in its entirety each of his thirty-minute lesson periods. The student, on his own time, may then replay his lesson in its entirety, hearing his voice and the teacher's comments over again. Instructors can follow a similar procedure in *speech classes.*

In a number of classes, much more class time can be devoted to real discussion than was ever before possible. This greater attention to individual comments by students—and to their questions—is possible because much of the basic subject matter content can be presented through *audio-tapes* plus workbooks. As a result students come to class better prepared for participating in a *discussion,* and the teacher has time in class for the discussion since some of the course content has already been given by tape. In some classes it is possible to record all of the basic course content for use out-of-class, thus freeing class time for discussion. And although a class may meet two hours a week instead of three, the students actually can get more personal attention in two hours of discussion with the teacher than they can by meeting with him three hours a week to hear lectures.

All these various means of individualizing instruction make it possible for a student to be freed from a set time criteria. He can "recycle"—i.e. he can take as many learning paths as he needs. And he can go over and over the content without embarrassment until learning mastery is achieved.

A caution and a reminder needs to be interjected. *Media is part of the system—but it is not the system.* It is the carefully programmed behavioral outputs which *is* the learning system. The desired outputs may be student initiated, teacher initiated, or mutually initiated and agreed to. The latter approach is generally the best approach, an approach "sealed" with a written contract signed by the learner and the learning partner (the teacher).

In a *Report of Instructional Technology,* the federal government, as never before, has shown concern with the output of the educational enterprise. Government thinking clearly indicates a thrust toward financial support of mediated instructional systems as evidenced by the report given by the *Commission on Instructional Technology* to President Nixon and Congress in 1970.

Efforts to use new technology in education will be largely wasted, according to the commission, if the technology is added to the educational process in a piecemeal way or is used merely to supplement traditional textbook and lecture methods of teaching.

"Technology, we believe, can carry out its full potential for education only insofar as educators embrace instructional technology as a system and integrate a range of human and nonhuman resources into the total educational process," the commission said in its report, *To Improve Learning.*

The commission was critical of the quality of education in the nation's schools and colleges, but it warned that technology would not be a panacea or a way to cut costs. The report also stated, "For all the fanfare, effort, money, and goodwill, the generality of schools and colleges is much the same as it was a generation ago."

The *National Institutes of Education,* whose establishment was recommended by the commission, are made up of several institutes that will make grants to universities and other independent research institutions, in addition to doing their own research. The commission report also proposed that the *National Institute of Instructional Technology* should:

1. Focus its efforts on research, development, and application in equipment, instructional materials, systems, and personnel training.

2. Consider establishing a library of educational resources to identify areas where there is a shortage of educational materials.

3. Help school and college libraries become "comprehensive learning centers," and stimulate interconnection and cooperative use of specialized libraries, data banks, and other school and college resources.

4. Support "demonstration projects designed to improve instruction through the wise exploitation of technology."

5. Encourage programs to improve the capacity of educators to make

most effective uses of technology, and programs to train specialists. Included would be programs to give administrators knowledge to manage technology effectively, to educate teachers in the most effective uses of technology, and to increase the number of qualified specialists in instructional technology.

6. Take the lead in bringing businessmen and educators together to advance the productivity of education through technology.

Furthermore, the commission saw the following benefits as resulting from incorporating technology in the educational process:

1. It should make education more productive by speeding up the rate of learning and helping teachers make better use of their time.

2. Technology could make education more individual. "Different combinations of teachers, students, materials, space, time, and dollars can respond more to actual learning needs and less to administrative convenience," the commission said.

3. It could give instruction a more scientific base by making reinforcement and reward a part of learning.

4. It could make instruction more powerful by making the educational experience more immediate and graphic to students through the use of films, recordings, and live or taped television programs.

5. It could make education more equitable by giving all students access to the materials and faculties that now are available only to students at the more affluent schools and colleges.

The report concluded: "The problems confronting American schools and colleges demand a cohesive, concerted attack. It is not the parts of the educational system that must be improved; it is the system in its totality. The key remedy is not computer-assisted instruction or team teaching or nongraded classes or educational parks or instructional television: it is innovations like these wisely integrated with each other and with teachers and the more traditional resources of education that may make the difference."

The commission has warned, however, that technology could be misused in education: "Unless technological means are harnessed to humane ends, with full regard for individual diversity and needs, no real benefit will accrue to society—indeed, the reverse is more likely.

From Library to Library-Media Center

The library-media center (L-MC) differs from the traditional library in its multi-media (and hardware) holdings and in the fact that more students are there on a directed study than on a leisure reading basis; i.e. more students are using the L-MC resources than studying the print of the textbook and the lecture notes of the instructor.

To understand the phenomenon of the positive transmogrifying changes occurring in today's libraries, a review of the last two chapters, summarizing the content in a different way, will vividly reveal the startling changes that have occurred over the past 5,000 years.

With the invention of writing the storage of useful knowledge took a sharp upward leap vis-à-vis what was possible (and what actually occurred) during the preceding one million years of man's existence on earth. Even after the invention of writing, the acquisition of knowledge accrued at a painfully slow pace over approximately 45 centuries until the invention of movable type in the fifteenth century by Fust, Gutenberg, Schoffer and others. In the century prior to 1500 Europe was producing books at less than one thousand titles per year. At that rate a full century would have been required to produce but one library of about 100,000 titles. By 1950, only four and a half centuries later, the rate had accelerated so sharply that the same Europe was producing 120,000 titles *a year*. What once took a century, by 1950 took just ten months! By 1960, only a single decade later, 100,000 titles could be produced in seven and one half months, and by 1970, world-wide production of titles reached 1000 per day, of which Europe contributed a third and North America about a tenth.

Paralleling the production of books has been the production of scientific journals and articles which have been doubling, like industrial production in the advanced countries, about every fifteen years. And according to biochemist Philip Siekevitz, "What has been learned in the last three decades about the nature of living beings dwarfs in extent of knowledge any comparable period of scientific discovery in the history of mankind." And Robert Hilliard, the top educational broadcasting specialist for the Federal Communications Commission, presses the point further: "At the rate at which knowledge is growing, by the time the child born today graduates from college, the amount of knowledge in the world will be four times as great. By the time that same child is fifty years old, it will be thirty-two times as great, and 97 percent of everything known in the world will have been learned since the time he was born."

Today the United States government alone generates 100,000 reports each year, plus 450,000 articles, books and papers. And according to the

Foreign Secretary of the National Academy of Sciences, Harrison Brown, on a world-wide basis scientific and technical literature mounts at the mind-boggling rate of some 60,000,000 pages a year, generated from more than 2,000,000 articles which are written by some 750,000 authors in fifty languages in approximately 35,000 periodicals. It is noteworthy that among these extant periodicals is the first scientific journal, *Philosophical Transactions,* first published by the Royal Society of London in 1665.

From the foregoing, library-media technologist Sol Cornberg's forecasting that reading and writing will become obsolete skills seems absurd. Yet, added to all this print material are equally, if not more potent, nonprint materials. Since 1950 nonprint learning materials have been produced at a rate even greater than print materials. With television and space satellites, the world truly has become a global village. An event in Chicago, London or Tokyo can be viewed simultaneously *while the event is actually happening* by 4 billion people, tied together as one human family, sharing in the curiosity, excitement, joy or sorrow of the telecast event. Thus Cornberg's forecasting that "reading will soon cease to be a *primary* form of information intake" becomes believable. Moreover, not only news and sporting events and moon walks are brought into our homes while they are happening but such educational programs as the *Undersea World of Jacques Cousteau, Electric Company,* and *Sesame Stree* Added to the marvel of commercial television are its derivations such as ITV, ETV, and VTR.

It can hardly be argued that every book, every television program, every film, every experience is a net gain for the advancement of knowledge. Nevertheless, we find that the accelerative curve in the production of print and nonprint materials does, in fact, closely parallel the rate at which man discovers new knowledge. For example, prior to movable type printing, only 11 chemical elements were known. The 12th chemical element, antimony, was discovered at the time of Gutenberg, 200 years after the 11th element, arsenic, had been discovered. Had the same rate of discovery continued, we should by now have had only elements fourteen or fifteen added to the periodic table. Instead, during the next 450 years, some seventy additional elements were discovered. And since 1900 we have been isolating the remaining elements not at a rate of one every two centuries, but at the rate of one every three years. The growth of language itself even more dramatically parallels the acquisition of knowledge. Of the 450,000 "usable" words in the English language today only perhaps 250,000 would have been comprehensible to William Shakespeare. Thus he would have been able to understand, on the average, only five out of every nine words in our vocabulary today.

Added to print and nonprint materials has been the development of the computer, a tool that can not only acquire knowledge, store it, and disseminate it, but can translate foreign languages into our own and can serve as an ever patient teacher (CAI). Coming into being at about the same time as television, computers have an unprecedented ability to analyze and disseminate extremely varied kinds of data in unbelievable quantities and at mind-staggering speeds. Computers have become a major force behind the latest acceleration in knowledge acquisition because of their potential as a research tool and for abstracting and storing useful materials on every subject, and because of their capability to produce print-outs upon demand. Combined with lasers, and other increasingly powerful analytical tools for observing the visible and invisible universe around us, computers have raised the rate of knowledge acquisition and its dissemination to dumbfounding speeds.

It should be plainly evident from the foregoing that those libraries of today that are exclusively print-oriented may join the one room school house as quaint memorabilia by the year 2000. There are a growing number of knowledgeable professionals today who recognize the fact that by the time the 21st century arrives there will be numerous libraries which will have more nonprint materials catalogued for circulation than print materials. The New York state public library system is already analyzing the prospects of the audio-video TV cassette supplanting the book as the number one item to be circulated during the last quarter century of the present millenium. Such cassettes likely will create an even greater revolution in the schools. Added to A-V cartridged cassettes will be the increasing use of individualized materials resulting from advances in offset printing and xerography, hand-held cameras and advanced video-tape equipment to produce one's own high quality films, tape recorders and walkie-talkies, and finally total sensoriums just now being glimpsed. With such variety, as Marshall McLuhan puts it, every man can be his own publisher. Such publication diversity and particularization will revolutionize learning.

In sum, libraries during the last quarter of the twentieth century will be unable to resist nonprint media. The change in schooling methods from mass teaching to individual learning, the demands for cartridged VTR lessons and programs by students and adults, and the further development of new nonprint media will force the change.

Though library-media centers, unfortunately, are not so much evolving from libraries because of leadership displayed by graduates of master degree programs, the changeover, nevertheless, is occurring. The impact of technological advances, which create insistent demands by students, teachers, and the general public for multi-sensory learning experiences, and which cannot be satisfied by the monosensory medium of print alone, is responsible. Out of fairness and reality, it should be pointed out that there *are* hearty "pioneers" in the library-media profession who are at the cutting edge of changeover from libraries to library-media learning centers. Some will be noted in subsequent chapters. Such leaders are to be found in every state in the land. And the ineluctable advances of technology will force the "timid" rest to "fall into line" by sheer user demand. However, print is *not* "dead." There still will be much print by the twenty-first century—but there will be newer as well as older forms of print material. However, the proportion of print material to nonprint materials as a form of information transmission will be *considerably* less in the year 2000 than was true in 1950. Television, the computer, and their off-shoots will see to that.

Those L-M practitioners who can grasp the significance of the multi-media, multi-sensory technological and social revolution now occurring at an ever accelerating rate can become the masters of new media rather than its reluctant captives. *Planning for* multi-media and its variegated uses, rather than having multi-media thrust upon a L-MC by patron demands, is an imperative. Indeed, perhaps what we need are "Councils for the Future" as Alvin Toffler suggested in *Future Shock* so that we are the managers rather than the victims of change. The L-MC is a logical choice to serve as the center for such future-oriented councils.

Practitioners in the education field (of which *all* audiovisualists and librarians, like teachers, are members) demand knowledge of research results facilitating learning. They must be able to judge not only the excellence of all types of learning materials, but their most appropriate use to create a conducive learning environment and to apply learning facilitation techniques.

Research results conclusively show that multi-media instructional techniques (by instructor or self) facilitate learning since the use of multi-media materials results in multi-sensory learning. Multi-sensory learning causes greater learner *activity* which psychologists have found not only enhances immediate learning but later recall. In short, the library-media center concept with its emphasis on a variety of realia, other multi-media materials, use of community resources, and activity rests upon a solid pedagogical foundation.

Perhaps *the single most important fact that the reader should learn from this text is that he should think of himself first and foremost as a teacher.* If one looks at himself as a "librarian" or as an "audiovisualist," the librarian is likely to be viewed by others as little more than a cataloger of books, and the audiovisualist is likely to be viewed by others as little more than a pusher of carts. The library should be considered a classroom and the audiovisualist and librarian the team teachers. When audiovisualists, librarians, and other professionals and paraprofessionals in the education field view themselves as teachers (and learners) they will *actively* seek out all manners of ways to create a "classroom" where they can be assured that learning is being facilitated and maximized. No good teacher will teach by books alone. Good teachers teach by providing their students with a variety of "nonbooks" and experiences as well as books— nor are the books limited to a single traditional textbook. Superior teachers, likewise, create environmental conditions where learning is enhanced in every possible way. "Audiovisualists" and "librarians" who can view themselves as *teachers* will find this shift in attitude and outlook resulting in a dramatic concomitant shift in a library's acquisition policies, its activities, and its environment. Such a shift in attitudes from bibliographer to teacher will result in the library becoming a true learning center.

Thus if the "librarian" and the "audiovisualist" think of themselves— and *act*—as teachers, greater self-respect, faculty respect, student respect, and community respect will result. This seemingly simple (but oh so difficult) shift of viewing oneself as a teacher will help result in the library becoming *the* center of learning for a school, college, university or community.

In succeeding pages, the emphases will be on media and learner characteristics in the school setting. But what is applicable there is also applicable with respect to the community library and the numerous and varied special libraries. The Tulsa County Public Library System with its guest lecture series, discussion groups, films, musicals, galleries of exhibits of all kinds, and community services programs is but one example of what excellent public libraries can and are doing. Likewise, such special libraries as the Lyndon Baines Johnson Presidential Library and the Henry Ford Museum are examples of superb special libraries which make abundant use of multi-media materials.

Pertinent research findings and characteristics of various type school and academic (postsecondary school) L-MC's will be discussed in subsquent chapters.

In concluding this chapter it is well to remember that a great teacher once viewed an innovation with great alarm. He said:

> *This invention of yours will produce forgetfulness in the minds of those who learn it, causing them to neglect their memory.*

The speaker was Socrates. He was talking about writing.

THE SCHOOL LIBRARY-MEDIA CENTER

Schools cannot content themselves with the time-honored process of stuffing students like sausages or even the possibly more acceptable process of training them like seals — John W. Gardner

Chapter 4 takes the reader from the past to the future, from older problems to newer ones, and presents some notable research findings. The chapter is concerned with what in many ways is considered the most challenging, demanding, and satisfying of all work—working with young people not yet wholly formed.

History and Development of School Libraries

The idea of placing a library in the school can be traced back to Europe. According to "Rapports des agents du ministre de l'interieur dan des departments," (1793) a small collection of books was to be placed in each school for the use of the pupils. This collection was to be under the care of the school administrator known as "Instituteur." By the latter 1800's there were more than a million volumes in the school libraries of France.

The idea of providing space, books and teachers in schools in America can be traced as far back as the 1630's to the West India Company in the Dutch colony of New Netherland. When the English seized New York in 1664 they did little to further the continuance of public education and libraries though in England the first school library had been established as early as 1606 in the Appleby Grammar School. However, book collections which already were in existence continued as collections in the private Dutch schools.

The French development of elementary school libraries mentioned above, did influence the United States during the early 1800's through New York Governor DeWitt Clinton's visit to Europe. It was Clinton's stay in France which caused him, no doubt, to place the school library in a position of prominence in his educational ideals. When Governor Clinton recommended the formation of better school systems to the

New York legislature in 1827, one of his proposals was that a "small
library of books should be placed in every school house." Though Clinton was outspoken in support of school libraries, it was not until 1835
that the voters of New York passed a law permitting school districts to
levy a tax specifically for library use. The school district libraries, as
they were called, grew rapidly. However, authority was granted in 1843
that permitted the library fund to be used for the purchase of school
equipment and payments of teachers' wages. At that time, 125 books
were the minimum recommended for the districts containing 50 children or less. After 1860, the number of volumes held by schools
steadily declined so that by 1874 the Twenty-First Annual Report of the
Superintendent of Public Instruction indicated only 831,554 volumes
in the entire state. In the same report, the superintendent recommended
the repeal of the law of 1835. Thus began a gradual decline of school
libraries in New York.

The development of libraries in New York was characteristic of school
library development in other Northern and New England states. During
the period 1835-1860, nineteen states passed legislation to promote
public school libraries. With the advent of the Civil War, schools and
their libraries were deprived of funds as well as personnel and facilities.
Thus, school library development was slow.

Room libraries were the prevalent type of book collections in 1900.
While some schools had been cooperating with public libraries to bring
library service to their pupils, others had purchased books from their
school funds and placed them in individual classrooms. The latter plan
was a common development in the elementary school; the teachers
favored the room library because they felt they could more or less super-
vise what the children read. In 1899, the National Education Association
had recommended that "A collection of fifty books in a room chosen
with reference to the age and ability of the pupils in that room is the
most satisfactory means of forming a taste for good literature."

A great turning point for elementary school library development in
the twentieth century came with the publication of the *Fourth Yearbook
of the NEA, Department of Elementary School Principals,* "Elementary
School Library Standards" 1925, and later published by the American
Library Association. It is evident that this publication paved the way
for the development of centralized elementary school libraries. Known
generally as the companion to the "Certain Report" (1925), elementary
school library standards were spelled out in full. Certain emphasized that,

Certainly no other factor in school organization bears more directly upon educational environment than does the library. When one considers how seriously a school may be cluttered up by the introduction of magazines and newspapers into classrooms, or how seriously work may be interrupted through haphazard introduction into a classroom of moving pictures, stereopticons, or victrola records, he will appreciate the importance of having a centralized agency for storing these materials where they may be readily available exactly at the time when they are needed.

The standards were very comprehensive, covering a definition of the library, a book collection, architectural specifications, administrative requirements, library instruction, budget, and a basic list of 212 books for the beginning elementary school library. It was Certain's opinion that no school was too poor to afford a centralized elementary library. Through his encouragement and practical illustrations of how a library can be organized with a few dollars, the development of elementary school libraries progressed. But one must not conclude as a result of the "Certain Report," every school in the nation set high priorities on school library services. This did not happen for several reasons; two of the most important being that during this period of time there often was no physical space available since few, if any, schools designed library space in their school building plans and few trained or untrained elementary school librarians were available. Furthermore the idea of paying for an "extra" staff member to be "librarian" was just too much to ask of most elementary school districts at that time.

The first financial incentive for elementary school library development came from the Carnegie Corporation in the early 1930's and was later supplemented by funds from the Julius Rosenwald Fund. Although much of the Carnegie support went for public libraries, the Rosenwald grants were directed toward development of Black elementary and high school libraries in the South.

For some time, despite the Certain Report and various financial incentives for school libraries, individual classroom libraries continued to be the norm. Even though, by 1940, statistics from the U.S. Office of Education revealed that there were 954 full-time elementary school librarians employed in the public schools of the United States with a total of 5,165 centralized elementary libraries in existence, there still remained slightly over eight percent of the schools (in the 94,254 elementary school systems in the United States) which had *no* type of library service at all.

Much the same situation occurred with respect to secondary school libraries. After 1900 those high schools having an enrollment of at least 200 students have generally been blessed with a library. However, up to 1925 it was unusual to have the library staffed. There was a small collection rather than a true library and whoever could spare the time "straightened up" the collection on a somewhat sporadic basis. From 1925 to 1950 the library was more likely to be staffed, but generally by an untrained clerk, parent or teacher instead of a trained librarian. It still happens in some places that the secondary school librarian is "last to be hired and first to be fired." Fortunately, since about 1950, this has been a rare occurrence.

In 1945, in *School Libraries for Today and Tomorrow,* the American Library Association published a national set of minimum recommendations for school library development. Although these guidelines were not detailed, they did present an organized approach toward school library development, and established standards for the development of all types of school libraries.

Even though definite progress in library development was made after the publication of *School Libraries for Today and Tomorrow,* the U.S. Office of Education issued in 1954 a statistical publication which alarmed the American Library Association, the American Association of School Librarians, the National Education Association, and the National Council of Teachers of English. It showed that approximately 75 percent of the elementary schools were without formal school library services. Although some classroom collections and other types of library service provided limited resources, there were millions of children without elementary school library services.

With the passage of the *National Defense Education Act* in 1958, funds were made available to both elementary and secondary schools for the primary purpose of building resource materials for various curriculum areas. Books and laboratory materials purchased with these funds had to be housed, supervised, and catalogued in accordance with the National Defense Education Act rules, and the administrator was held responsible for knowing where all materials purchased with these funds were located. Most elementary schools did not have libraries. This meant make-shift adjustments had to be made within many schools to accomodate the materi

The *Standards for School Library Programs,* published by ALA in 1960 set forth the basic requirements needed for truly functional school library programs in the form of both qualitative and quantitative standards. They were worked out by representatives from the *American Association of School Librarians* and representatives from twenty other professional and lay organizations interested in quality education for children and youth as well. These standards have been used as guides in most states in evaluating existing library conditions and in formulating long-range plans for library development. Additionally, many states have formulated their own standards based on regional standards and the American Library Association's standards.

Tremendous growth in school library development began in 1965 with the *Elementary and Secondary Education Act.* This act virtually doubled the amount of federal aid available to public schools. There were five provisions in the bill. Title I provided funds for local school districts through state education agencies, which educated children from low income families. Title II authorized distribution of funds to the states for acquisition of library resources, including textbooks and audio-visual materials. Title III provided grants to local school districts for the establishment of supplementary education centers. Title IV made funds available for development of regional educational research and training facilities. Title V provided funds to strengthen State Departments of Education.

The Elementary and Secondary Education Act of 1965 has produced a faster growth of school libraries than any previous stimulus. This growth resulted in greater quantity and quality of library materials and the development of school library standards in many of the fifty states. It also resulted in the establishment of some centralized school libraries and funded the appointment of state school library supervisors in many states. Upon the expiration of the Elementary and Secondary Education Act, solid foundations will have been made by State Departments of Education, as well as local school districts, for the establishment of school libraries in every school district in the country.

In 1966, according to the U.S.O.E. *Digest of Educational Statistics,* there were 73,216 elementary school systems, with 31.4 percent having central L-M facilities. U.S.O.E. statistics also indicate that more than 20,000 school districts in the United States and its possessions have received federal funds since 1965. Not only have there been new materials placed in school libraries, but the number of qualified librarians on the elementary level has also increased. There was, however, a severe shortage of personnel. To meet these shortages, many colleges offer specialized course work to prepare school librarians. Several of the colleges accredited by the American Library Association provide graduate work in which one may specialize in the area of school librarianship. Along with this program there are similar offerings for preparation as instructional materials special- ists. Wide offerings also exist in the two-year colleges for those who aspire to multi-varied paraprofessional positions.

The new *Standards for School Media Programs,* published in 1969 by ALA provides school systems with quantitative recommendations for the major resources and facilities and equipment for school libraries serv- ing all grade levels, kindergarten through 12. In general, the same recom- mendations apply to elementary, junior high, and high schools. These recommendations integrate the entire instructional resources of the school into a centrally administered school instructional materials program. Al- though resources, facilities and equipment recommendations are well identified, other aspects of the total administrative and organizational structure of the instructional materials program are less detailed and hence are less recognizable as recommendations. These "standards," used in conjunction with the "1906 standards," provide rather high goals for which schools should strive. The standards are beginning to have a measur- able impact on the development of library-media centers.

Philosophy of the School Library-Media Center

It is important that every L-MC consider a formal statement of philoso- phy which should contain three parts: 1) the general philosophical state- ment explaining the theoretical basis for the L-MC; 2) the long-range pur- poses which identify the major phases of service that will be rendered in fulfillment of the philosophy; and 3) broad objectives which designate types of service and identify the role of the director. It should be realized that such a philosophy cannot be developed without some understanding of the clients to be served and of the staff itself. Nor without this under- standing can intelligent policies and procedures evolve.

Many school districts have school L-M supervisors who are responsible for the L-M development in all the schools in the district; in such cases, the supervisor has the responsibility of development of the philosophy for his district. He may work on a continuing basis for implementation of the philosophy with the school administrator, teachers, and parents who may form a standing committee.

If there is no one school district L-MC supervisor, one of the local librarians should make it his job to establish a small (generally five are enough) committee to work out a philosophy and continue as a standing committee.

If the L-MC is to become the true center of education and learning it is most important that it be based upon a true understanding of the needs and background of its clients—and of the development and understanding of the educational processes.

The school librarian has children who come not only from middle and upper class homes, but from homes where no reading matter at all is available except perhaps for an occasional comic book or a *True Story* type magazine. Here lies the real challenge. The professional library-media worker has an unprecedented opportunity to help decrease the future dropout rate of those from educationally deprived homes. It is a conclusive fact that the single greatest cause of school dropouts is the inability of the student to effectively read. Library-media specialists can mitigate this serious deficiency.

Middle-class school teachers, librarians, and other learning specialists must set as their highest priority adjustment to the needs of those students in their charge most unlike themselves. The student typical of a middle-class WASP home does not need as much care, attention and direction as does the youngster who comes from the ghetto. Such youngsters desperately need compensatory education. Above all else, this means acquiring the skills to functionally read.

To assist the child who has come from a functionally illiterate home often requires the "patience of Job" and the "love of Jesus." But it must be done if our country is to ever see its bright promise.

Those who choose to work in school libraries must *actively* seek out the young people who need the most help. They can become library helpers and pages. They need more story hours so as to instill a love for books and reading. They must have their appetites so whetted that they *just have to* learn how to read well. It is highly advisable that the L-M professionals either has first been a teacher (and at several different grade levels) prior to becoming a librarian—or obtain such experience subsequently. This point is consistent with what has been argued previously in that the teacher and the librarian and the audiovisualist need to more nearly merge their knowledges and skills. Teaching experience enables the L-M professional to *know* how to teach reading, *know* the curriculum, *know* the problems the teacher is faced with in his classroom. Such understanding and rapport will facilitate student learning.

School L-MC's need to be open at least half an hour before classes begin in the morning so that children can come in to check books in and out. Likewise it should be open for at least an hour after the last class has been dismissed for the day. Moreover, *the school L-MC should be open every Saturday for at least four hours.* Few school L-MC's in the country are open to students on Saturdays or school vacation periods. But they should be.

The typical pattern of most school L-MC's is for a class to come to the L-MC anywhere from once a week to once a month. This is not enough! If the L-MC is to become an integral part of the learning experience for its students, and if it is to serve its local community as it should, then it needs to be open to its students before and after school and on Saturdays and school vacation periods as well. The extra salary costs for the year for such service would be far less than the costs of a half time professional. The building and media already exist.

During summer vacation periods, in particular, it is essential that the director of the library-media center take the initiative to identify, and bring to the center, children from its lowest income areas; preschoolers beginning at age three should be brought in for story hours, films, slides, tapes, picture looking and for letter identification and sounds. Children of school age who have been identified as having reading problems need to be made pages and to assist in other library work under adequate supervision. The "better" readers should be enlisted as tutors for the "poorer" readers. Sufficient research has been compiled to indicate that to "teach one" is one of the best motivators for improving one's *own* skills. Utopian—yes. Idealistic—yes. Necessary—yes!

Too often, information specialists have seen their roles as passive, as responders rather than as creative initiators. They provide the service *when asked*—but do not determine *what is needed* and then do something about it. The middle-class child will ask for help—sometimes. The economically handicapped child often does not even know the questions to ask—and if he did he wouldn't ask them anyway. This is because he all too often senses that his teacher does not feel comfortable around him because he does not fit into the life-style mode of the adult who could help him. Ghetto children may be economically and educationally deprived—but they aren't "dumb." They are often highly sensitive and cannot be fooled. When genuine, no-strings help is extended they will eagerly grasp the help extended. When they sense a stiffness, or a holding back, that youngster is lost and he and society are both worse off because of it.

Those aspiring to positions in the school library, library-media center, media center, learning resources center, learning center—or whatever— should not choose this specialty area unless they are sincerely dedicated and committed to initiating meaningful programs leading to the development and expansion of reading skills—and the love and pursuit of knowledge. There are employment opportunities for both the professional and paraprofessional who welcome these challenges.

It is not intended in this short treatise to provide all the practical methods and technical skills needed to perform the functions required in a school L-MC. These skills will be acquired elsewhere. The intended purpose of this chapter simply is to provoke the reader into considering "Is this the level of librarianship I wish to work on?" However, a passing mention of specific skills which need to be acquired maybe helpful. They include: instruction to students on the physical location of materials; the classification system; the use of the card catalogues; the use of dictionaries; the use of reference books and materials; story telling; reading methodology; psychology of learning; chart and poster and exhibit making; management; selection of materials for both research and recreation; ordering; processing and cataloging; working with faculty and administration. School library-media technologists must remember that the faculty needs an annual preschool opening orientation session. New sources of information and materials and their locations need to be reviewed; the latest audiovisual equipment needs to be demonstrated; the services which are offered need to be emphasized.

As important as this annual orientation program is, it is not enough. Each center needs a standing LM-C committee composed of administrators, teachers, older students, as well as the L-MC's director. As we have discussed, one of the chief responsibilities of the library-media center's staff is to *sell and motivate faculty* to use the multivaried resources of the center. By working with faculty—on a constant and continuing basis—the L-MC staff will aid in generating excitement and learning within the school.

Students' avocational interests need to be ministered to as well as their needs for classroom assignments. One of the best ways of doing this is to work in conjunction with the guidance department. Most registration forms have the students' interests recorded. If not, ask that new forms include this information. Note the reading scores and grade level as well.

Wouldn't it be a pleasant surprise for the student to receive a letter (it could be a form letter with appropriate empty spaces to personalize it) which stated that the director had noticed so and so's interest in, for instance, *astrophysics* and as a result wanted to call to his attention a new book that had just come in on the subject? Such reaching out by the staff helps the center to become a true learning center.

The L-MC's staff can take the leadership, or assist, in identifying and helping poor readers. It is an unfortunate fact that few library-media staff members see this as any kind of role for them. A *Tutor's Club* consisting of the school's best readers—whom they should be able to recognize since these few students are responsible for the majority of circulation—can be sponsored by the L-MC. They should be enlisted in helping the poorer reader. Using poor reading students to help even still poorer reading students is also a motivating means not to be overlooked for as Joseph Joubert said, "to teach is to learn twice."

Facilitating Teacher Facilitation of Student Learning

There *is* an increasing awareness by many concerned teachers and administrators that the text/lecture and the talk/chalk method of imparting knowledge are not the only, or the best, means for facilitating learning. Also, there is an increasing awareness of the effectiveness of programmed instruction and the writing of explicit, measurable learning objectives, and that when students are given greater responsibility for their own learning they *do* respond intelligently, imaginatively, relevantly, and responsibly. Evidence of this fact are "issue oriented" research questions generated by English students for two secondary school teachers.

One English teacher asked her class what topics would be interesting research questions. She received suggestions such as the following problem posing questions:

- —Should schools educate for marriage and family life?
- —Should there be a guaranteed income for everyone?
- —How is society dealing with the mentally ill?
- —Is the black power movement a danger to the social structure?
- —Should federal aid be given to all schools—public and private?
- —Is the population explosion a serious threat to survival?
- —What are the roots of prejudice of all kinds?
- —How should the problem of drug addiction be handled?

—Should the standard work week be four days?

A World History teacher using the same challenging teaching approach as the English teacher above received from his students such provocative questions as the following:

—Is Communism a threat to world peace?
—Why did the U.S. send troops to the Dominican Republic?
—How was Castro able to come to power?
—Has the U.N. outlived its usefulness?
—Is it possible for permanent peace to ever come in the Middle East?
—Is the United States an imperialist nation today?
—Can East and West Germany be reunited?
—Is the policy of apartheid in South Africa in any way defensible?
—What was behind the Soviet invasion of Czechoslavakia in 1968?
—What are the similarities and differences between our government and the governments of Canada and Mexico?

Both the English teacher and the history teacher cited above were doing "problem solving" of "issue oriented" teaching. The problems were those perceived to be relevant *because the students formulated them.* To solve a problem requires research. To do research requires an adequate multimedia collection and the assistance of able, library-media technologists.

What an opportunity this approach affords for meaningful, individualized learning, and what an exciting challenge for library-media technologists who have the opportunity of working in such a setting.

The simple but imaginative and effective teaching techniques reported above point up an important role of the school L-MC director and his staff. Not only must the L-MC staff cooperate with such advanced teaching techniques but they should encourage (with enthusiasm) others to try new methods with their help. The cross-fertilization of ideas that result can strengthen the entire teaching/learning process in the school—and the students become the benefactors. And that is what education is all about.

There are, of course, a number of other things that an "activist" L-MC staff can do to facilitate teacher facilitation of student learning. Among them are:

—Invite teachers to the center at the beginning of the new school year

for a "tea and orientation." At that time the teachers should be taken
on a guided tour of the L-MC. Materials should be pointed out, broad goals
for the year spelled out, suggestions made as to how the center can supplement and/or be a part of the teaching/learning process, questions an-
swered, and suggestions and recommendations solicited from those present.

—Notify teachers of new media. One of the best ways of accomplish-
ing this is through a regular monthly "L-MC Bulletin" distributed to the
entire staff. The bulletin can cite major new acquisitions, services provided, and such news as faculty projects which make substantial use of
the center and/or staff. In between issues of the montly bulletin particular media which has arrived can be brought to the attention of particularly
interested faculty through a personal note, or better still through personal contact.

—Place interesting magazine and periodical articles of interest to the
teachers' academic area in his faculty mail box. Not only might such
articles be helpful to the teacher in his work, but such thoughtfulness
is likely to cause greater utilization of the only truly interdisciplinary
learning center on campus, the L-MC.

—Maintain an "Innovations Center" in which new equipment and materials for facilitating learning is displayed. Such a center need be nothing
more than an alcove. It should, however, be a comfortable place. A
couple of easy chairs, a percolating coffee pot, and a coffee table are
enough to set the desirable atmosphere. The director, or a member of
his staff, can point out new programmed instruction materials, audio
cassettes, video cassettes, new projectors, professional materials on how
to write measurable performance objectives, and the like. A comfortable
place will facilitate a lively discussion in a nonthreatening atmosphere.
This may result in a learning facilitation idea being taken away by the
visitor to the betterment of his students. The monthly L-MC bulletin
can serve as the general vehicle to inform the faculty of "new media"
available in the "Innovations Center." "Buttonholing" individual faculty
members is also legitimate! L-MC staff must be salesmen. They should
be proud of their wares and services and not ashamed to advertise what
they have to offer.

—Place a form in each teachers' school mail box each month to ascertain what L-MC assignments are being planned for the students. Teachers
should not be "dunned" if they do not respond. It will only irritate them.
But a monthly request serves as a gentle reminder which not only will

facilitate L-MC usage, but which will also make it possible for the center staff to plan ahead, and hence provide more efficient and qualitative service.

Facilitating Student Learning

Implicit in this, and previous chapters, is the fact that the individual teacher is the chief motivator of student usage of a center's materials and resources. The research results reported later will conclusively point up this fact. What has already been suggested with respect to facilitating *teacher* facilitation of student learning is therefore most important. The *most* important task of library-media technologists is "selling" the faculty on the full, positive use of the L-MC and its staff. It will be more effective than trying to "sell" students directly. *Yet,* there are many ways and means of reaching young people irrespective of the faculty. These also are important; good professionals and paraprofessionals leave no stone unturned.

What then are some of the things that an "activist" center staff can do? Following are a few suggestions which top-flight practitioners have found successful when working directly with students:

—Get to know the students' interests and go to them actively with suggestions rather than waiting for questions. By planning with the counseling staff or with the English department in secondary schools, or with the self-contained classroom teacher in elementary schools, an interest inventory form can be prepared for the student to fill out. The center should have a copy of this form, if not the original, in one of its files. This file should be actively used so that students are as aware as teachers that the L-MC is there to complement and supplement the teaching/learning function of the faculty. Most students will respond positively when singled out for personal attention in positive ways.

—Encourage library aids to read new books. They often are the best "sellers" of new acquisitions. Some L-MCs keep a special alphabetical file by title of reviews by students in a prominent spot in the L-MC. Pages especially like to be "book reviewers." Students take delight in reading reviews by their fellow students. In elementary schools pages like to go to the various classrooms in the school in accordance with their own approximate grade levels to make oral book reports to the class. Students respond positively to such student book reviewer visits.

—Help students learn *how* to use all of the equipment, materials, and reference sources of the center. This is equally true for teachers, perhaps even more so. We will not use what we are embarrassed about not knowing how to use. Periodic workshops before school, during school, and after school must be provided in which the demonstrator *must* assume that the student (or teacher) knows *nothing.* But demonstrations are not enough. The "workshop" participants must be provided the opportunity to also demonstrate that *they* can successfully make use of the equipment, materials and reference sources of the center. Teaching continues by the L-MC staff until learning mastery is achieved.

—Encourage the leisure time use of audiovisual equipment and materials. Unless the potential user of audiovisual equipment and materials knows how to use them he will remain just that—a potential rather than an actual user. When this first hurdle is overcome, as described above, the next step, obviously, must be to have sufficient variety of resources and materials to fulfill user needs. Basically, this requires that as much attention be given in budget allocation and selection of nonprint material as to print materials. Moreover, the same ease of retrieval of nonprint materials through cataloging as for print materials must receive high priority. Special attention should be given to the acquisition and cataloging of video cassettes since such cassettes hold particularly high promise for wide future usage. In short, if as much consideration, care, and attention is given to the nonprint as to the print collection, and if patrons know how to use such materials, relatively good usage of nonprint to print materials can be expected.

—Organize a book club, library assistants, and/or audiovisual club. Students like to belong. In too many schools there are insufficient activitie for those bent on intellectual or mechanical pursuits. Both are possible in the L-MC. Moreover, such organizations will attract both boys and girls. All the L-MC director need do is to announce in bulletins, put a notice on bulletin boards, and tell teachers and students when and where the first meeting of each will take place. A number of conscientious students will appear. The Book Club will attract the readers. The Library Assistants Club will attract not only readers but *workers*—and potential future L-MC paraprofessionals and professionals. The Audiovisual Club will attract the mechanically minded doer. Most all will also prove to be the L-MC's best public relations ambassadors. Each group will add to the stature of the L-MC as well as adding to their own intellectual and emotional growth. A conscientious effort must be made constantly by the center's staff to help young people to learn and enjoy reading and to develop judgment in selecting worthwhile print and nonprint materials.

The Center as a Coordinating Agency

The effective L-MC, by whatever name it is called, is a coordinating agency. It is (or should be) the center of learning of any given institution. It is a common meeting ground for both students and teachers. For the learning center to be effective, its director needs to not only have the ability to administer and organize and know about books and media, but to understand the philosophy of education. Furthermore he needs to like and understand both teachers and students and know how to stimulate their interest and cooperation.

Examples of Modern Library-Media Centers in Education

The English Primary School

Probably the better English primary schools and their offshoots in North America (most notably the elementary schools of North Dakota) provide the best examples of what is advocated in this book. Children enrolled in these schools typically range from five to twelve years of age. The English primary school has been placed "inside the Library." The school *is* the library and the library *is* the school.

The conviction and philosophy of the English primary school is that learning is likely to be more effective if it grows out of what interests the learner, rather than what interests the teacher. This is a truism to any adult: we know how quickly we can learn something that really interests us, and how long it takes to master something that bores us, or for which we have a strong distaste. The English primary schools and their offshoots elsewhere are "informal," "free," and "open" vis-à-vis the "formal," "quiet," and highly "structured" traditional schools. Though learning under this informal system evolves from a young person's interests it is not an abdication of adult authority, only a change in the way it is exercised. Thus informal teaching requires that students receive firm but understanding guidance from their teachers. The teacher has the responsibility to structure the learning environment for his students in the best possible way, and to help it change and grow in response to each child's evolving interests and needs. The teacher's role is not passive. He knows clearly what he is trying to do and how and why. He must help each individual child learn how to think, to form judgments, to discriminate.

The Plowden Committee, largely responsible for reforming English primary education, defined the teacher's task as providing "an environment and opportunities which are sufficiently challenging for children and yet not so difficult as to be outside their reach. There has to be the right mixture of the familiar and the novel, the right match to the stage of learning the child has reached." This declaration is as apt to L-MC technologists as to classroom teachers.

Like the teacher, the L-MC technologist's role must consist of far less telling and there must be far more doing on the part of the student. Jean Piaget, internationally renowned child psychologist, argues children must be presented with situations that encourage them to experiment, to manipulate things and symbols, trying them out to see what results they produce. Formal operations or verbal abstractions for most children should not begin before age twelve.

"The principal goal of education," Piaget insists, "is to create men who are capable of doing new things, not simply of repeating what other generations have done—men who are creative, inventive, and discoverers," who have "minds which can be critical, can verify, and not accept everything they are offered."

This requires for children up to about age twelve that schools and libraries need to provide an abundance of concrete materials they can explore, manipulate, and handle—materials they can play with, for play is a child's work. Indeed, Piaget and other child psychologists note that *play is the principal means of learning in the wonder preteen years.*

The informal schools demonstrate in practice what John Dewey, America's foremost giant of educational philosophy, argued in theory: that a deep and genuine concern for individual growth and fulfillment not only is compatible with but indeed demands an equally genuine concern for cognitive growth and intellectual discipline, for transmitting the cultural growth and intellectual discipline, for transmitting the cultural heritage of the society.

To enter an informal classroom for the first time is a disorienting experience—even for experienced educators. As examples of activities of informal classrooms are presented in succeeding pages, the reader is asked to view the setting *not* as a classroom per se—but *as a library, an L-MC, or a learning center.* Note the possibilities for reforming a traditional classroom, a school library, an entire school, or the children's section of a public library.

As one enters an informal classroom, be it in Leicestershire, England or Grand Forks, U.S.A., one is immediately struck by the fact that the classroom does not *look* like a classroom. Rather it looks like a workshop in which "interest areas" take the place of the familiar rows of desks and in which individualized learning has replaced what English educators now disparagingly call "the talk and chalk" method, i.e., the teacher conducting a lesson for all the children simultaneously from his vantage point at the chalkboard lining the front side of the classroom. The most prevalent example approximating this model of informal schooling in Canada and the United States are kindergarten classrooms. However, not even the richest Canadian and American kindergartens have the incredible wealth and variety of materials found in just the average informal English primary school (and their offshoots elsewhere).

The visitor will note that the reading corner is an inviting place with a rug or piece of old carpet on which children may sprawl, a couple of easy chairs or perhaps a cot or old sofa for additional comfort, and a large and tempting display of books at child's height. The math area typically will have several tables pushed together to form a large working space. On the tables, in addition to a variety of math texts and workbooks, will be a box containing rulers, measuring tapes and meter sticks, strings, and the like. Other boxes containing pebbles, shells, stones, acorns, bottle tops, pine cones, and anything else that can be used for counting, along with more formal mathematical materials, such as Cuisenaire rods, Dienes blocks, Stern rods, and Unifisc cubes will be present. Also present will be several balance scales, with boxes of weights, rocks, water, feathers, and anything else worth weighing and comparing.

Near the mathematics area there likely will be a large table-height sandbox and another table-height water table which comes "equipped" with an assortment of empty milk cartons, bottles, pitchers, plastic containers and the like, all with their volume (¼ liter, ½ liter, liter) marked on them. There may also be an oven; following a recipe for cookies or muffins provides still another application of simple mathematical notions, along with practice in reading. L-M technologists should keep in mind that just as the reciting of words is a form of reading so is the comprehension and use of the international languages of mathematical symbols and musical notes as well as various other art forms. "Reading" should not, and must not, be thought of only as prose. To limit a library only to prose-type reading and books, therefore, is to limit students' access to all of man's communication materials and possibilities.

Nearby the math area will be a crafts area consisting of various tools, "junk" (so marked), i.e., empty cereal, egg and other cartons, paper towel and toilet rollers, cardboard, pieces of wood, scraps of wallpaper and fabrics, cigar boxes, tagboard—in short, anything children might enjoy using to construct things. Somewhere nearby (or out in the hall) will be easels and jars of paints and brushes for painting. A playhouse and adult clothes for young children also are likely to be seen.

There usually will be a music area somewhere in the room with castanetes, cymbals, drums, xylophones, records, and other (sometimes homemade) instruments. There will be a science area with rocks and shells, leaves and other local flora, candles and jars, perhaps some small motors, batteries, bulbs, and wire. In all probability, there will be several animals—hamsters, a kitten, a rabbit, a turtle, white mice, or hatching chicks from an incubator.

Space for as many as forty children is provided by replacing desks with a smaller number of chairs and tables, by using closets, cloakrooms and hallways.

A visitor accustomed only to formal classrooms is likely to be disoriented also by the sound and movement of an informal classroom even more than by its physical arrangements. At any one moment, some children may be hammering and sawing at a workbench, some may be painting or playing musical instruments, others may be reading aloud to the teacher or a friend, still others may be curled up on a cot or piece of carpet, reading in solitary absorption, oblivious to the sounds around them. (They belong to a generation, after all, that does its homework with the "telly" or a radio blaring away.)

Elsewhere in the room, moreover, there are likely to be children seated at a table or sprawled on the floor, writing a story (children in informal classrooms do a prodigious amount of writing). Other children may be determining how many more grams a shoebox full of sand weighs as compared to a shoebox full of feathers. Others may be measuring the perimeter of the classroom, one another's height, the length of a visitor's shoe, and writing it all down. And so it goes. And always there is the sound of children talking—to themselves, to their friends, to the teacher, to visitors (in sharp contrast to formal classrooms in every land where children and visitors usually are carefully segregated from one another).

The sound and movement are not limited to the classroom itself. There is a continuous ebb and flow of children into and out of the room—into the halls and corridors, the cloakrooms and other classrooms, the lobby and library.

Understandably, in view of all the sound and motion, the first impression
may be one of chaos. But as the visitor becomes acclimated to informal
schooling, it becomes clear that the activity and the noise that flows from
it usually is purposeful. It also becomes clear that the teacher has far
from abdicated his roll. He always seems to be in motion, always to be
in contact with the children—talking, listening, watching, comforting,
chiding, suggesting, encouraging—periodically taking time to jot down a
comment in the record book he keeps on each child (James is trying to
write his name for the first time, Susan is making much brighter pictures,
Peter seems to be resisting "maths," Evelyn has learned to multiply by
three, John is coming out of his shell—he talked more easily and played
with others for the first time. . .).

In well conducted informal classrooms, one becomes aware, too, of the
sense of structure. For all the freedom the children enjoy, for all the ease
and informality, for all the child-centeredness, there is no ambivalence
about authority and no confusion about roles.

Because informal schooling results in the combination of great joy,
spontaneity, and activity not surprisingly self-discipline and relaxed
self-confidence are natural accompaniments. It is almost impossible to
find a disruptive or restless child operating under the philosophy of informal schooling. The self-fulfilling prophesy of expecting children to be-
have properly produces the expected behavior; understanding children's
needs and giving them the same courteous treatment one gives to one's
own peer group results in the children responding in kind. This is not to
suggest that every English child is perfectly adjusted; like every country,
it has its share of emotionally disturbed children. But the warmth, support, concern, and care evidenced in informal schools, and their flexibility in handling children according to their own individual needs,
seems to mitigate the behavior problems that emotional disturbance
produces.

As for achievement of children enrolled in informal schools as compared to formal ones, standardized tests reveal that those children enrolled in informal schools do at least as well in the basic "3 R's" as those
enrolled in formal schools. This is a major achievement in itself for products of informal schools have accomplished this not through joyless ex-
trinsic coercion but through joyful intrinsic liberation. Not only do the
products of informal schools do as well or better in the basic 3 R's as
the products of formal schools, but they stand out in a variety of other
areas as well, e.g., spoken and written English, drawing and painting,

listening and remembering, care and skill, ingenuity, moral judgment,
neatness, handwriting, general information, ability to concentrate on
an uninteresting task, breadth and depth of out-of-school interests, and
the ability to successfully work with others.*

In sum, central to the informal English primary schools is a view of
childhood as something precious in its own right, something to be
cherished for itself and not merely as preparation for later life.

Fortunately, the philosophical concept of the English primary schools
has been imported by North America. Of all places on the continent,
none is making such rapid progress in introducing the concept into its
schools as the state of North Dakota. There, nearly every elementary
school in the state has converted over to the English informal system
of schooling.**

The perceptive reader will realize that this brief discussion of the
philosophy of informal schooling represented by the English primary
school and the elementary schools of North Dakota has profound implications for library-media technologists, too. It should be obvious
that books alone are totally inadequate as a medium of knowledge
transmission in school and public libraries. Not only should there be
books, records, films, audio and video cassettes, playback machines, and
projectors, but small motors, microscopes and science equipment for
experiments, small animals and fish, weights and measures, mathematical
materials (math is the *favorite* subject of most students enrolled in informal classrooms), musical instruments, art supplies, a radio, a television
set, etc. The monomedium library of books then can become the multi-
media library-media center in recognition of the fact that learning is
not acquired through reading alone. There already are a growing number of schools that recognize this fact. The L-MC's of the elementary
schools of Flossmoor, Illinois represent but one outstanding example
of the dynamic role that such centers can play in the entire learning program of a school system.

Does the L-MC really have to be a "shhh" place? Does an L-MC really
need so many hard wooden tables and chairs? Would it really be so
heretical to have a few comfortable overstuffed chairs and sofas? Would

*D.E.M. Gardner, *Experiment and Tradition in Primary Schools,* London: Methuen,
1966.
**Vito Perrone's and Warren Strandberg's forthcoming publication *The New Way
to Look at School* (Linnet Books, Hamden, Conn.: 1973) vividly describes the exciting developments occurring in that state and elsewhere in the United States and Canad

it really be so heretical to have one or more comfortable rugs for youngsters to sprawl on? Would young people be more attracted to an L-MC
having a wide variety of materials, an informal atmosphere where they
could talk rather than whisper (or less), where they could lounge and
sprawl in comfortable chairs or lie on a rug, where they could eat an
apple vis-à-vis today's formal school and public libraries? Does today's
typical school and public library *really* present a facade of welcome—
or is it rather quite the opposite with its collection of books and its
artificiality of super silence? Is the suggestion of creating informal libraries as well as informal schools really so heretical? The reader is left
to ponder this question in light of our knowledge of motivation, learning, and mental hygiene.

A Learning Center in Action

Flossmoor Junior High School in Illinois recently purchased a 15-
minute, eight millimeter film with accompanying tape on pollution.
This is hardly unusual—except for the fact that the film's producers
were two of its own eighth grade students.

In operation since the fall of 1970 the Media Center, as it is called,
has evolved from a collection of books in a single classroom (1960) to
its present multi-media collection which occupies a space equivalent to
five classrooms.

Approximately half of the area houses print materials, a reference
room and a developmental reading room. The remaining half houses
the audio-visual learning aids, where students work with filmstrips,
film loops, tapes, records, slide transparencies, microfilm readers, a cal-
culator, and a four-channel FM wireless receiver. The Media Center provides a student with tools for research and offers diversified ways for
him to learn. The center is coordinated with the total academic program
and is used to supplement classroom goals. The director of the Media
Center, Peggy Hall, succinctly sums up the philosophy of the center by
describing it as a "learning laboratory."

Tutorial assistance for students who need special help is another important concept of the center. Every teacher of an academic subject is
assigned to the center for 50 minutes each day, so that there are always
at least four teachers available for coaching in English, math, science,
and social studies.

The school's principal, Donald Barber, notes that the idea of every
teacher being responsible for every student is part of a changing orienta-

Nonprint materials are widely used by students in the Learning Center to individualize instruction at the Flossmoor Junior High School in Illinois. Photo courtesy of STAR Publications, Chicago Heights, Illinois.

tion in schools today. The closed classroom with its lock-step patterns is giving way to a variety of combinations—team teaching, seminars, tutorials, independent study, to name a few. What is emerging is a less rigid, more human school atmosphere focused on the individual rather than the institution.

The center's math assistance program (MAP) illustrates Principal Barber's observation. If a child has missed school during the presentation of a necessary concept, or if he has not been able to grasp it during class time, his teacher can refer him to one of the specially designated MAP teachers. Here he is able to get instruction on a one-to-one basis until he catches up. Thus, the flexibility of the Flossmoor program—and the attitudes that govern it—let the class progress without losing the individual.

The kinds of assignments that teachers make also has been affected by the Media Center. An entire class, for example, no longer works simultaneously on a given general topic. Sometimes there are not more than 10 books on a topic, if even that, let alone enough for an entire class. So assignments are staggered or varied to make maximum use of the materials available, and to avoid the frustration and anxiety which occurs when a student cannot find what he needs.

Themes, term papers, or notebooks are no longer the only ways to report on a project. The boys who made the film on pollution are a case in point.

So, too, is the student who used the center's Kodak Visualmaker to make slides illustrating the American Revolution. According to Mrs. Hall, this student had never achieved recognition for his written work, but this project was successful enough to send his classmates scurrying to the center to explore similar presentations.

With the increasing emphasis on studying contemporary problems, teachers who used to shun magazines and pamphlets as reference sources are now encouraging their use. Magazines are often the best and sometimes the only sources, for studies on Appalachia, urban and racial problems, drugs and other modern social concerns. For this reason the center keeps a microfilm file dating back to 1965 on the 15 most frequently called-for magazines.

As the teachers have become more familiar with materials and equipment, the range of assignments and activities has steadily increased. Daily duty in the center gives teachers a chance to learn more about what is there, and to explore what can be incorporated in classroom programs.

Nothing is bought for the center unless it has been previewed by the department the purchase would most likely affect and then only after assurance is given that the item purchased will be sufficiently used to justify the expenditure.

The Media Center, which may have from 30 to 150 students in it at various periods, operates with a staff of four—a librarian, an AV assistant, a clerk, and a director. However, student volunteers help out—50 library aides who work during their resource periods, and 35 boys who have carefully been trained to operate the equipment that is loaned out to classrooms.

Mardell Parker, district superintendent, asserts that learning centers are one answer to the recognized need for more individualized instruction. But he also notes that the learning center concept must be coupled with others such as open schools and the bringing of more volunteer adults into the schools.

All seven of the Flossmoor schools have developed learning center concepts—concepts which integrate print, nonprint and human resources into a viable cybernetic model of instructional excellence. Though the Flossmoor model is not widespread, there are nevertheless a number of notable examples of L-MC centered learning in every state in the land.

Some Studies in the Use of School Libraries

Five High Schools Study

During the fall semester of 1966 this writer undertook an investigation of library usage in five high schools. Four of the high schools in this study were located in California and one was a United States Department of Defense dependents' school for children of American military personnel serving in the Tokyo area of Japan. There were four spaced out sampling periods of one week in length to determine the purpose of withdrawals by the students. Study the High School Library Use Questionnaire reproduced here before proceeding further with the reading of this chapter. The readers' attention is also drawn to the *Survey of High School Libraria* appended to the end of this chapter; the results are reported throughout the text.

Table 2 [p. 76] is very revealing for a number of reasons. It should command the attention of current and future practitioners. It will be noted that high schools A-D, the four California high schools, reveal an identical pattern of usage. Better than 97 percent of each high school's library col-

HIGH SCHOOL LIBRARY USE QUESTIONNAIRE

☐ Male   ☐ Female

CLASS STANDING (check only One box)

☐ 1. 9th grade

☐ 2. 10th grade

☐ 3. 11th grade

☐ 4. 12th grade

TYPE OF WITHDRAWAL (check only One box)

☐ 1. Book

☐ 2. Periodical

PURPOSE OF WITHDRAWAL (check only One box)

☐ . For class work

☐ 2. Not for class work

IF WITHDRAWAL IS FOR CLASS WORK ANSWER QUESTIONS BELOW:

_____   _____

Name of Class and Number   Instructor's Name

MAIN purpose for which withdrawal is being made (check only one box)

☐ 1. Term paper of notebook

☐ 2. Paper (other than a term paper or notebook)

☐ 3. Speech, oral report, debate or panel discussion

☐ 4. Test (other than a speech)

☐ 5. Test (speech)

☐ 6. Class discussion

☐ 7. Book report

☐ 8. Other (specify)

TABLE 2

PURPOSE OF WITHDRAWAL WITH THEIR MEDIA
CHARACTERISTICS IN FIVE HIGH SCHOOLS

High School	Percent for Class Work	Percent not for Class Work	Percent of Withdrawals Which Were Books	Percent of Withdrawals Which Were Periodicals	Percent of Withdrawals Which Were Nonprint
A	97.5	2.5	97.3	2.4	0.3
B	97.4	2.6	97.3	2.7	0.0
C	98.0	2.0	98.0	2.0	0.0
D	97.5	2.5	97.4	2.6	0.0
E	52.9	47.1	99.2	0.8	0.0

lection serve classroom assignment purposes. Contrast this with the American dependents' high school library in Japan in which less than 53 percent of the withdrawals are attributed to classroom assignments.

At first glance it might be said "but the American dependent's high school students do not have access to public libraries so they therefore are more heavily dependent upon their high school library for recreational reading." This argument does not hold up well under closer examination, however, for there is a military base library which is stocked basically with recreational reading. Admittedly though, it is geared more for the post high school adult than high school students. Nevertheless, there are wide reading choices of the latest novels as well as older classics.

There are several characteristics which do make this American dependents' high school unique, however, compared to high schools located within the United States. Cars are not allowed American high school students in Japan and no American television is available. These two factors certainly not only explain in part the distribution of reading between class demands and recreational reading needs, but also explain the fact that the highest withdrawal rate per student of all five high schools also occurred in this overseas American high school.

The results of this investigation may lead one to assume that television (and cars) have had a negative effect on the reading habits of our youth.

One must be careful and exercise caution with respect to extrapolating this finding into a generalization, however. For one thing, the purpose of the investigation was *not* to compare the reading habits of television viewers versus nontelevision viewers. Secondly, this was only a single example, and thirdly what is *gained* as well as what is lost by viewing television has never been adequately ascertained. Perhaps it is true, as the results strongly suggest, that television and the mobility of our youth have decreased the amount of reading which they do. On the other hand, perhaps what they see in pictures and hear in sound may be at least equal to or even more educative than the same amount of time spent in reading.

Table 2 also reveals certain other notable characteristics of high school libraries and their students. Without any exception, better than 97 percent of all withdrawals at all five libraries were book withdrawals. Less than 3 percent of the withdrawals in any high school were periodicals and, indeed, only one high school had any nonprint withdrawals. This indicates that records, tapes, films, filmstrips and other audio and video materials (in 1966) were practically nonexistent in these five libraries or what was available was either not allowed to be checked out or perhaps there was no demand for the use of nonprint materials made by the faculty. Certainly in no sense could these libraries be considered L-MCs.

Tables 3 and 4 reveal, with but little exception, that the lower the class standing the greater the demand placed on the collection. These results are remarkable for several reasons. Studies made by Harvey Branscomb, Patricia Knapp, Errett McDiarmid, and the author have all revealed the reverse insofar as colleges and universities are concerned; that is, the seniors borrow more materials from the library than juniors, juniors more than sophomores, and they more than freshmen.

The explanation for this anomaly is not easily found. Perhaps, again, mobility may have something to do with it. If in *Table 4* the statistics did not include the American overseas high school, in which students have no cars, there would be *no* exception to the findings that the *lower* the class standing the greater the use of library materials. A thesis would be very much in order to (1) determine if similar results would be obtained in another study *and* followed by an in-depth study to determine *why* freshmen borrow more than sophomores, sophomores more than juniors and juniors more than seniors. Such an investigation may reveal a statistically significant correlation between obtaining a driver's license and a drop in reading. Such an exploration could be expected to result in significant findings with respect to the differences in reading habits between various classes.

Table 5 clearly reveals that the single most significant factor causing high school students to use the library collection is to make book reports. This contrasts with several studies of college students which reveal that assignments of term papers is the chief impeller for the use of media housed by their library-media center. Second in importance, but far down in need as compared to book reports, are term papers and other papers which are about equal in importance with respect to the demands placed upon the collection.

The results shown in *Table 5* are revealing in several other areas as well. As will be noted, little demand is placed on the collection for speech tests, tests, or classroom discussion. These results are also in contrast to studies of demands on the library collection by colleges. Perhaps greater heterogeneity in academic ability at the high school level, in contrast to the college level, accounts for such disparity. Whatever the reason or reasons, it is worth examining the validity of such an assumption.

"Why should a library collection serve mainly as a resource for provid-

TABLE 3

CLASS STANDING AS RELATED TO THE USE OF LIBRARY MATERIALS AT FIVE HIGH SCHOOLS

High School	Percent of Withdrawals Accounted for by Freshmen	Percent of Withdrawals Accounted for by Sophomores	Percent of Withdrawals Accounted for by Juniors	Percent of Withdrawals Accounted for by Seniors
A	31.5	29.8	23.0	15.7
B	43.0	28.1	18.7	10.2
C	49.5	32.8	6.8	10.9
D	38.0	14.8	28.1	19.1
E	52.4	14.8	12.1	20.7

TABLE 4

CLASS STANDING AS RELATED TO THE TOTAL WITHDRAWALS GENERATED BY STUDENTS IN FIVE HIGH SCHOOLS

Total Withdrawals	Percent Accounted for by Freshmen	Percent Accounted for by Sophomores	Percent Accounted for by Juniors	Percent Accounted for by Seniors
2686	37.4	24.3	17.7	20.6

TABLE 5

ASSIGNMENT DEMANDS CAUSING STUDENTS TO WITHDRAW
LIBRARY MATERIALS AT FIVE HIGH SCHOOLS

High School	Percent Accounted for by Term Papers	Percent Accounted for by Other Papers	Percent Accounted for by Oral Classroom Work	Percent Accounted for by Speech Tests	Percent Accounted for by Nonspeech Tests	Percent Accounted for by Class Discussion	Percent Accounted for by Book Reports	Percent Accounted for by Other Class Work
A	5.4	6.8	6.2	0.8	0.4	1.7	61.9	16.8
B	11.3	6.1	3.4	0.2	0.0	1.1	68.2	9.7
C	12.9	6.7	15.2	0.0	0.5	1.1	53.1	10.5
D	5.2	3.1	4.2	0.0	0.0	0.0	62.1	25.4
E	19.3	21.4	10.4	0.4	0.0	4.2	32.4	11.9

ing materials for book reports? If this is the purpose of a high school library, are high school libraries needed at all? Certainly, books for book reports could more inexpensively be obtained from the public library or by the purchase of pocket books from book stores. To have student withdraw from 32 to 68 percent of their needed materials from the library for book report purposes makes one wonder what is being taught in the classrooms. Book reports are essentially "busy work" in most instances. Certainly, there are exceptions if a careful analysis is made of a work, but this is usually not the case. The usual case is for the student to include in his book report (1) the title, (2) the author's name, (3) description of main characters, (4) description of the most exciting or interesting part, and (5) was the story liked—why or why not? Book reports may be legitimate assignments for elementary school youngsters, but for students in grades 7-12 such an assignment, in most instances, is questionable at best. The school library should serve as a research center to conduct research, not as a center to serve up pap for ill conceived book reports. Maintaining a simple reading record within the center proper though can have value. Such a record can serve as an aid to others who may be considering checking out a particular book. It can assist in developing critical evaluation skills. This is a functional approach with a specific objective and thus can be justified.

Table 6 shows, almost without exception, that English classes make the greatest demands upon the collection, followed by social studies and natural sciences. Though this may seem a logical order, the same does not necessarily hold as consistently true for colleges and universities. Again, one wonders, if enough research oriented tasks are assigned in other areas of the high school.

Knowing from the discussion above that the chief use of high school library materials in this study was to make book reports, it is not a surprising revelation to find in *Table 7* that more than 71 percent of the entire withdrawals are attributed to English classes. *Table 7* reaffirms the fact that book reports are also the chief assignments causing students in English classes to withdraw books from the library. It is noteworthy, in consideration of the topic in hand, that an investigation of a middle-school in Illinois, serving an affluent community, revealed that 52 percent of the withdrawals were fiction and 48 percent of the withdrawals were nonfiction. This division between fiction and nonfiction is *not* atypical—though further research is required to say so with any degree of certainty.

It will be noted from *Table 7* that the chief withdrawal impeller for

TABLE 6

RANKED SUBJECT AREAS MAKING THE GREATEST DEMANDS ON THE LIBRARY COLLECTIONS AT FIVE HIGH SCHOOLS

High School	Agriculture	Art	Business	English	Health	Languages	Math	Music	P.E.	Natural Sciences	Social Studies	Tech. Studies
A	5	5	9	1	4	—	5	5	10	3	2	10
B	—	5		1	—	4	5	—	5	3	2	—
C	—	—	—	1	—	—	—	2	—	3	3	—
D	—	—	—	1	—	—	—	—	4	3	2	—
E	—	—	5	1	6	—	—	—	—	3	2	4

PERCENTAGE OF, AND CHIEF REASONS FOR, WITHDRAWALS FROM THE LIBRARY COLLECTION ATTRIBUTED TO ENGLISH, SOCIAL STUDIES AND NATURAL SCIENCES AT FIVE HIGH SCHOOLS

High School	English	Chief Withdrawal Impeller	Social Studies	Chief Withdrawal Impeller	Natural Sciences	Chief Withdrawal Impeller	Total Percentage	All Other Subjects
A	71.1	Book Reports	14.9	Book Reports	7.9	Papers Other than Term Papers	93.9	6.1
B	79.1	Book Reports	13.4	Book Reports	5.5	Term Papers	98.0	2.0
C	79.1	Book Reports	6.2	Oral Reports	6.2	Term Papers	91.5	8.5
D	79.7	Book Reports	15.9	Book Reports	2.9	Papers Other than Term Papers	98.5	1.5
E	72.9	Book Reports	20.2	Term Papers	4.7	Term Papers	97.8	2.2

social studies classes is not as uniformly consistent as it is for English classes. Nevertheless, even for social studies classes, book reports are the assignment most responsible for the circulation of high school library materials. Only in the natural sciences, of the three most significant library demand areas with a high school, do other types of assignments dominate.

On average, it can be readily seen, the subject areas of Engish, social studies and natural sciences account for better than 95 percent of all withdrawals from the high school library collection. Just the English and social studies area alone, on average, account for about 90 percent of the collection withdrawals.

There are a number of tentative conclusions which can be drawn with respect to this data. Most important, there is the obvious fact that in the schools studied in 1966 the high school teachers were textbook oriented in their teaching approaches rather than research oriented. Moveover, there is no reason to believe that secondary school teaching has changed much since then. For students to gain a perspective of their subject matter from a single point of view is questionable at best. But it may legitimately be asked what about teacher effectiveness? Is there any relationship between teacher effectiveness and student use of library materials? The answer to this question needs much attention. It is difficult to get at because of the reluctance of evaluators to cooperate in such an investigation.

However, there is one study which this writer was able to conduct concerning this question which, as far as is known, is the first such report ever made of teacher effectiveness as related to high school student use of library materials.

The principal of one of the high schools cited in the Five High School study agreed, independent of knowing what circulation statistics would reveal, to evaluate his 24 faculty members for the research conducted, with the obvious understanding that his school or staff not be identified. The results of this pioneering effort are most revealing.

The three teachers ranked by the principal among the top ten percent of the staff in the high school accounted for 89.7 percent of all withdrawals from the library during the four sampling periods! Of the three teachers ranked by the principal in the lowest 10 percent with respect to teaching effectiveness not one of their students checked out a single book during the four sampling periods! Of the four members of the faculty ranked as exactly average only one caused his students to check out library materials. Finally less than half, only 9 out of 24 teachers, caused their students to check out at least one work during the four one-week sampling periods.

One of the librarians who participated in the *Five High Schools Study* provides revealing insight in a letter she wrote to the investigator: "We have several particularly 'gung-ho' teachers who are for projects—group and individual. It's made a huge difference. Then there are those who see no use for using the library while teaching Julius Caesar in sophomore English!"

Obviously, the above reported results must be cautiously treated. The high school was small. It was only one high school. Perhaps the most glaring weakness of all is the evaluation procedure itself. The study, as noted, relied solely upon a single evaluator. It would have been more valid to have also had the evaluation of teaching effectiveness made by each instructor's own peer group and most importantly, the students themselves. As ideal as this would be, it is not a practical means for obtaining such data at this time in most places. Faculty would not cooperate in such a venture and students likely would not be allowed to. Thus a heavy dependence on evaluation, of necessity, must be placed elsewhere. During the investigation, only one of the five administrators was willing to "stick his neck out" in the name of research. One principal wrote "This is confidential information, of course, and we are not authorized to furnish information of this sort on our staff." His response was typical of the others. Such reluctance is understandable. But such information, for research purposes, is badly needed so that the L-MC can more adequately meet the needs of all its students.

Student Attitudes Toward Learning

In another study, consisting of 150 sophomore students in an Illinois high school in 1971, students reported they were bored with high school classes that emphasized the following:

−Lectures and taking notes
−Memorizing
−Going strictly by the book
−Irrelevant films
−Teachers who do all the talking

In response to the question as to what an "Ideal Class" is like, these same 150 sophomores wrote:

−Allowed to learn on your own
−Allowed to work in the library
−Work on research projects

—Work on independent interest and study projects

—Take more educational field trips

Certainly, the above attitudes strongly suggest a central role for the L-MC. It is the responsibility of the L-MC staff to report such findings to the faculty and then work as a team to more adequately meet the needs of the students.

Happily, the students' concept of the "Ideal Class" is not a mirage or an illusion never to be attained as has already been reported with respect to English primary school education.

Summary

In summary, the L-MC's staff must create a sensitivity and an awareness among its students, teachers and administrators of the value of the L-MC so as to further the development of a civilized society. The staff must be action oriented rather than passive. This requires not only seeking out the good readers but the poor readers. It means not only aiding the progressive teachers but the traditional teachers (lecture and text/talk and chalk). It means that the thrust is people oriented rather than object oriented. Policies and procedures are aimed at making the L-MC the humane heart of the institution. Working there is both a challenge and an opportunity.

The strong individualizing trend we see occurring in education has been facilitated by the philosophy of the open classroom and the aid of the computer. The computer makes it possible to schedule classrooms, teachers, and students more flexibly than ever before. The computer makes it easier for a school to cope with independent study, with a wider range of subject offerings, and more varied informal activities. Richness of materials and activities, along with CAI, PI, and other techniques radically enhance the learning possibilities through diversity inside and outside the classroom. They permit each student to advance at his own pace. They permit him to follow a custom-cut path toward knowledge, rather than following a rigid syllabus as in the traditional classroom, a room which now is beginning to rapidly fall by the wayside. A good deal of education in the future may take place at hours of a student's own choosing and in the L-MC. There vast libraries of data should be available to him via computerized information retrieval systems, with his own tapes and video units, his own laboratories, and his own electronically equipped study carrel. In short, education is increasingly coming inside the L-MC.

SURVEY OF HIGH SCHOOL LIBRARIANS

March 23, 1966

TO WHOM IT MAY CONCERN:

I am doing a doctoral study on the community college library with particular reference to the Library at College of the Desert.

It has been recommended by my doctoral committee that I determine what instruction, if any, students received from our local high schools in how to use the library. I would greatly appreciate it if you would therefore answer the following questions:

1. What specific instruction in how to use the library, if any, do students receive in the 9th grade? By whom?

2. What specific instruction in how to use the library, if any, do students receive in the 10th grade? By whom?

3. What specific instruction in how to use the library, if any, do students receive in the 11th grade? By whom?

4. What specific instruction in how to use the library, if any, do students receive in the 12th grade? By whom?

5. What particular strengths do you see in your over-all library program?

6. What particular weaknesses do you see in your over-all library program?

7. Do you believe your students have sufficient knowledge in how to use a junior college library without the necessity of further instruction by the junior college staff? Why, or why not?

8. Additional comments

I thank you most sincerely for assisting in this doctoral study.

A stamped, self-addressed envelope is provided for your convenience.

Sincerely,

Richard W. Hostrop, Investigator

THE TWO-YEAR COLLEGE LIBRARY-MEDIA CENTER

*The love of learning opens the doors of knowledge and oppor-
tunity for all people—*Anon

The two-year college has been called the greatest social invention of the
twentieth century. This type of institution, above all other institutional
types of higher education, is a true "People's College." Its open door
policy enables every youth to "have a try" at postsecondary education.
Not only are liberal arts offerings at the freshman and sophomore levels
comprehensive but there also are wide technical and vocational offerings
of one and two years in length. Because of these conditions, the challenges
and opportunities afforded by the two-year college to library-media
technologists are as varied as they are interesting.

Beginnings, Settings, and Working Conditions

Considering that the two-year college often called "junior college" but
increasingly called "community college" or just "college" is only about
seventy-five years old as an institution, its growth has been phenomenal.
In 1900 there were no two-year colleges—by 1972 there were more than
1,100 such institutions in the United States and 125 in Canada—each
with a L-MC. Moreover, one new two-year college has been opening
every week in North America for the past decade.

The first two-year college library was established at the first two-year
college, Joliet Junior College (Illinois), in 1901. Because the two-year
college has had a comparatively short tradition and the physical plant is
more modern, its library-media center is often most imaginative. It is
more likely that a unified system of book and nonbook media will be
found in such institutions than on the older and more traditional four-
year college and university campuses. In addition the growth of two-year
colleges mentioned above means that there are excellent job opportunities
for those who have had anywhere from one year of paraprofessional
training to advanced preparation from a university. Thus the employment

Delta College Library, University Center, Michigan. Photo courtesy of the college.

Chabot College Library, Hayward, California. Photo courtesy of the college.

outlook is excellent through the 1970's for library-media technicians as well as for graduates of professional graduate programs. Graduates of two-year college programs will be in particularly strong demand with an annual need of providing the services needed for the more than three million students enrolled in two-year colleges alone.

Reports, Studies and Research Findings

In spite of the two-year college's relatively short life much attention to its development has been paid. The first comprehensive reporting of the two-year college library was by B. Lamar Johnson in his noted 1939 book, *Vitalizing a College Library*. At the time he wrote this classic, Doctor Johnson was both head Librarian and Dean of Instruction at Stephens College which was then a two-year college for women. (He retired as Professor of Higher Education at the University of California in Los Angeles in 1972.) Doctor Johnson's dual role at Stephens College resulted in the library serving as an important means of individualizing instruction at Stephens College.

There have been a number of studies made investigating various aspects of the two-year college library-media center. However, most of these studies have been concerned with quantitative rather than qualitative standards—although the two have often, unfortunately, been assumed by researchers to be synonymous.

Norman E. Tanis and Milton Powers in *College and Research Libraries* (vol. 28, #5)* reported an important investigation under the title, "Profiles of Practice in the Public Junior College Library." In their study they reported certain quantitative results of six well established institutions. The data revealed is noteworthy and is reported below:

MEDIAN BENCHMARKS FOR 1963-64

Number of volumes at the end of year	22,500
Number of volumes added during the year	2,427
Number of volumes withdrawn during year	250
Number of periodicals being received at end of year	287

*Reprinted with permission of *College and Research Libraries*.

Number of hours of student assistance 2,668

Number of professional personnel (FTE) 3.0

Number of nonprofessional personnel (FTE) 3.0

Total library expenditures (excluding capital outlay) $55,200

Salaries $34,819

Wages .... $ 3,262

Books and other library materials $14,453

Binding .... $ 813

Other expenditures .... $ 1,941

Hours per week library was
open 64

Total square feet assigned to
library 13,084

Stack areas 2,500

Seating areas 6,350

Staff and work areas 1,413

Other areas 2,300

Expenditures for library per
FTE Student .... $ 19

Expenditures per FTE faculty
member .... $ 549

Expenditure ratio of total library
expenditures to total institutional
expenditures (excluding capital outlay) ... 3.7

Extrapolation revealed:
Books per FTE Student 9.4
Books per FTE Faculty 180

The authors propose that these median benchmarks, updated each year, could possibly form the minimum quantitative threshold standard for adequacy in public junior college libraries throughout the United States. Public junior college libraries falling below these benchmarks, unless special circumstances in their local situation justify a temporary lower level of performance, would be in danger of giving inadequate service to their students and faculty.

Tanis, in another article, "Strengthening the Junior College Library: The Application of Standards" for *College and Research Libraries* commented that, ".... one of the most fruitful ways of strengthening a junior college library through the use of the ALA Standards is by applying them in a rigorous self-study. The standards should be utilized as guides, and the quantitative criteria should be treated as 'benchmarks' derived from desirable practices of comparable junior college libraries."

Tanis further reported in the same article that "During the past five years, the standards have been used by institutions for the purpose of self-study. There have been interesting results. Here, summarized, are many of the reports that have come to the Association of College and Research Libraries Committee on Standards:

1. These self-studies, which have utilized the standards as important tools of evaluation, have demonstrated definitely that there exists a real need for better communication between the library, the faculty, and the administration.
2. These evaluations provided insight into the very great diversity of demands that are placed upon the library of a two-year college; very often it was found that the budgetary provision for the library lagged far behind the demands for services.

The report concluded that those who took part in a self-evaluation were unanimous in their opinion that the evaluation was followed by action.

The most comprehensive study of the two-year college library since *Vitalizing a College Library* came 29 years later. In *Teaching and the Community College Library* this writer reported an in-depth study of one public two-year college library at College of the Desert in California. Some notable conclusions which emerged from this study were:

1. Student use of library materials was largely course stimulated.

2. Library facilities were chiefly used as a study hall.

3. Studies of senior institutions indicated that more than half of their loans are made from the reserve collection, whereas reserve loans at College of the Desert amounted to less than 12 per cent. On the other hand, two-year college students borrowed from the general collection at the rate of 18.96 loans for the academic year, as compared to an average of approximately 12 loans per year reported for senior institutions.

4. An analysis of titles of books most frequently borrowed revealed that less than 25 per cent of such titles were available in paperback form.

5. More than 75 per cent of the departments were essentially nonlibrary dependent for instructional purposes.

Table 8 reveals that the library user, at least insofar as College of the Desert is concerned, achieves higher academic success than the nonuser. Similar studies bear out this contention. It must be borne in mind, though, that the differences in this, and similar studies, have not been *statistically* significant.

TABLE 8

ANALYSIS OF CUMULATIVE GRADE-POINT AVERAGES FOR SELECTED CATEGORIES

Category	*Mean*
Female	2.54
Male	2.37
Total Students	2.44
Female Library Users	2.54
Female Nonlibrary Users	2.51
Male Library Users	2.41
Male Nonlibrary Users	2.25
Total Library Users	2.46
Total Nonlibrary Users	2.32

The analysis of student characteristics of library users and nonusers at College of the Desert revealed the following:

1. Students who were older than the student population as a whole were likely to be nonlibrary users.

2. Library-media users, both female and male, were more likely to be residing at home than were nonlibrary users. More female than male students lived at home, and females borrowed more library-media materials per capita than did male students.

3. Students who achieve greater scholastic success in high school than the college student population as a whole were more likely to be L-MC users than nonusers.

4. Students who achieved greater scholastic success in college were more likely to be library-media users than students who did not do as well scholastically in college.

5. Students who carried heavier unit loads in college were more likely to be library-media users than those who carried lighter unit loads.

An analysis of statistical results at College of the Desert, derived through the chi-square formula, suggests several statistically significant dependencies or relationships in two-year colleges:

1. *Sex and withdrawals of books from general collection:* Females borrowed more books from the general, open-stack collection than did males.

2. *Fall units completed and withdrawal of reserve books:* Students who complete more units of work withdraw more reserve books.

3. *Cumulative units completed and withdrawals of library-media materials:* Students who complete more cumulative units withdraw more periodicals and reserve books, and make more total loans, than those who complete fewer cumulative units.

4. *Number of books in home and reserve books withdrawn:* Students who report having the greater number of books in their own homes withdraw more reserve books.

5. *Socioeconomic status and total loan withdrawals:* Students who are placed in higher socioeconomic strata, based upon their fathers' occupations, make greater total (periodicals + reserve books + books from the general collection) withdrawals than do students of lower socioeconomic status.

No statistical significance was established in the *College of the Desert Study* for the relationship of quantitative borrowing of library-media materials to the following characteristics: Sex (except for books from the general collection); Age; Marital Status; Living Situation; Number of Persons in Household; Scholastic Aptitude; High School Attended; High School Grade-Point Average; Fall Semester Grade-Point Average; Cumulative Grade-Point Average; Fall Semester Units Completed (except for reserve books); Cumulative Units Completed (except for periodicals, reserve books, total loans); Major in College; Use of Public Libraries; Number of Books in the Home (except for reserve books); Number of Periodicals Subscribed to; Socioeconomic Status of Students (except total loans); Average Weekly Hours Worked for Pay.

Table 9 is particularly interesting because it summarizes those six courses of 165 offered at College of the Desert which were responsible for placing the greatest demand upon the total library-media collection.

It will be noted that each course listed in Table 9 above is ranked in the upper 15 percent for total withdrawals. A similar characteristic prevails with respect to loans per student. As clearly noted, these courses were the six highest ranked courses in the college with respect to the percentage of students enrolled who withdrew materials for course usage.

TABLE 9

RANK OF SIX COURSES ON THREE SCALES OF USE OF THE TOTAL COLLECTION

Course	Total Loans	Rank	Loans per Student	Rank	Percent Withdrawing	Rank
Technology 33	27	25	9.00	1	100.00	1
Health 8	90	13	4.50	4	95.00	2
Geology 1A	75	15	1.50	25	94.00	3
Drama 10A	32	21	2.66	9	91.67	4
Philosophy 6A	91	12	4.55	3	85.00	5
Speech 2	69	16	2.15	13	81.25	6

Interviews with nine faculty members, three of whom were both library-dependent and library-related instructors, were carried out as part of the *College of the Desert Study.* Theirs were the six classes which generated the highest in-breadth L-MC usage and the six that produced the greatest in-depth usage. Together, they represented 23.68 percent of the thirty-eight full-time instructors who taught one or more graded classes during the fall semester of the 1965-66 school year at the college. It is note-worthy that seven of the classes were in the English and Speech Division, two were in the Engineering and Technology Division, and one each represented the divisions of Health and Physical Education, Physical Sciences, and Social Sciences.

The interviews clearly revealed that these nine instructors considered the L-MC an essential adjunct to the instructional program, and that they themselves were positive factors in impelling the use of its materials. Certain characteristics of instructional approach were common to all. The assignments given were generally spelled out very explicitly, and frequently the students were provided with specific references to guide their selection of materials. The instructors continually followed up on the assignments made, and informed the students of their progress. Frequent class discussion of students' reading also appears to have played a major role in stimulating L-MC usage. Emphasis was placed upon proper elements of research—the selection of numerous source materials, adequate

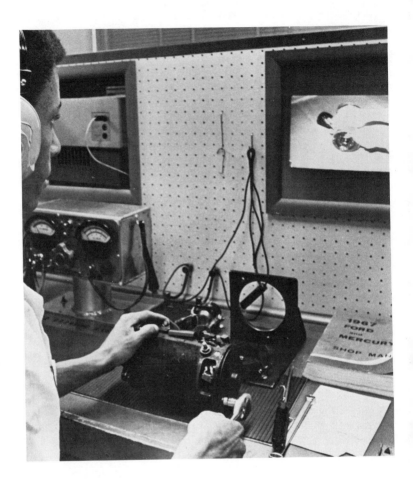

This simple-to-build carrel uses rear screen projection to utilize the unique capabilities of 3M Company's Sound-on-Slide System. Sound and picture cannot get out of phase. Student can replay slide or slides until he understands the subject. Photo shows Central Piedmont Community College, Charlotte, N.C., Auto Mechanics Program under the direction of Claud Hunter. Photo courtesy of the college.

footnoting, and the compilation of a suitable bibliography. Indeed, actual practice in *how* to use the L-MC was an important course objective of some instructors. All of them, however, maintained high classroom standards and did not hesitate to inform the students that they expected library work to be of high quality.

Finally, the interviews left the impression that library-impelling instructors were themselves fond of books, which suggests the likelihood that in some part this attitude proved infectious to some students.

Table 10 shows the results obtained from questionnaires mailed out to students enrolled at College of the Desert in 1966.

TABLE 10

PURPOSES OF IN-LIBRARY USE AND TIME SPENT IN SUCH USE, 320 FULL-TIME STUDENTS REPORTING

Purpose	Average Hours	Percent of Total In-Library Use Time
Studying out of textbooks	5 h., 45 m.	50.0
Working on term papers	2 h., 25 m.	21.1
Research	1 h., 22 m.	12.0
Reading for examinations	1 h., 07 m.	8.7
Personal or recreational reading	0 h., 56 m.	8.2
Total in-library use 11 h., 35 m.		100.00

There seems little question that a foremost, if not the chief, purpose of in-library use at College of the Desert was as a place to study textbooks. In regard to course-related uses of the Library, Table 10 reveals that more than half the time was spent in research connected with the writing of term papers. Thus it would appear that term papers constitute the predominant factor for impelling students to use the L-MC for course-related work.

Heavy borrowers of library-media materials who were interviewed at College of the Desert appeared to have certain characteristics in common. The chief reason impelling their use of library-media materials was term paper assignments. The course most frequently mentioned as being responsible for extensive reading was English/Speech 1A. This finding was not surprising for statistics previously reported, as well as the results of interviews with library-impelling instructors, clearly revealed that English/ Speech 1A to be the most significant course at College of the Desert in terms of involving many students in library activities. It is notable that among the heavy borrowers of L-MC materials many students had grade-point averages below 2.00, although a few had grade-point averages above 3.00. It is also notable that a majority of the students reported they would have continued to use the L-MC even though no specific assignments had been made—albeit, they admitted, at a reduced volume of use. Planned majors apparently had little influence on the extent to which materials were used. Finally, it appears that heavy borrowers of L-MC materials were inquisitive—they "thirsted" for knowledge, even though that knowledge might not have been directly translated into better grades.

Straight A Students. There were five full-time students who made straight A's during the fall semester of 1965. Aside from achieving straight A's these five students had other characteristics in common, too. First, they were older than the average full-time student, whose mean age at College of the Desert at that time was 19.54 years. For the 4.00 students it was 27.40 years; although, because of the few cases, the median would perhaps present a more accurate picture at 22 years. Second, they were all L-MC users, although one student did not use the L-MC at College of the Desert. Third, the students strongly agreed that term papers was the method most effectively used by instructors to impel student use of the L-MC. They were in general agreement also that elimination of most instructors' requirement of term papers would eliminate the use of the L-MC, for term papers were about the only kind of assignment requiring library materials. Fourth, all of the students had completed thirty-eight or more semester hours in addition to being 4.00 students; therefore, their opinions had a measure of "sophistication" beyond that of the average student at College of the Desert. All of these students' cumulative GPA's in college were above 3.00.

It is perhaps worthy of mention that none of the Straight-A students showed special academic promise in high school, as revealed by the fact that their high school GPA's made them ineligible for university entrance at the time of graduation. Indeed, one student was a high school dropout.

During the fall of 1969 Kenneth Allen investigated the library-media center in three Illinois two-year colleges ranging in full-time student enrollment from 596 to 2,286. He reports in his book (*Use of Community*

College Libraries, Shoe String Press, 1971), the following results from 1,312 student questionnaire responses from selected classes from the three colleges:

1. 74 per cent indicated that utilization of the library was necessary for academic success;

2. 72 per cent indicated the resources of the library met their needs;

3. 50 per cent responded that utilization of the library affected their final grade;

4. 72 per cent responded they used other libraries in the community in addition to those of the colleges;

5. 30 per cent responded that they entered the library daily, 46 per cent weekly, 16 per cent monthly, and 8 per cent never entered the facility;

6. 51 per cent listed their major reason for coming to the library was to study without using library materials, 35 per cent to use library materials, 8 per cent to check out materials, 4 per cent to use audio-visual materials for independent study, and 3 per cent to find a friend;

7. 32 per cent had made the most use of the library for the social studies division, 26 per cent for humanities, 22 per cent for occupational, 17 per cent for mathematics and science, and 3 per cent for physical education;

8. 60 per cent indicated they had consulted the librarian for assistance at some time.

Faculty questionnaire responses (194) consisted of the following:

1. 71 per cent indicated their teaching techniques were affected because of a lack of library materials;

2. 62 per cent indicated they required their students to use the library;

3. 45 per cent indicated they currently had books or audio-visual materials on reserve in the library.

Seven College Study

During the 1966–67 academic year an investigation of the contribution made to learning by the library-media center in seven two-year colleges was conducted by this writer and is reported here for the first time. In the *Seven-College Study,* one college was located in New York, another in Missouri, another in Kansas, and the remaining four were located in California. All seven colleges had been in existence for at least ten years. Tables 11 through 16 and 20 through 21 summarize the findings of this investigation.

TABLE 11

COURSES, PURPOSES, AND TYPES OF WITHDRAWALS IN WHICH
20 OR MORE TRANSACTIONS OCCURRED DURING FOUR
SAMPLING PERIODS IN FOUR TWO-YEAR COLLEGES
(N = 347)

Course	Main Withdrawal Purpose	Type of Withdrawal
English Composition	Term Paper	General Collection
U.S. History	Nonterm Paper	General Collection
Photography	Term Paper	General Collection
Oil Painting	Term Paper	General Collection
History of the West	Term Paper	General Collection
Fundamentals of Data Processing-Lab	Term Paper	Periodicals
Introduction to Chemistry	Test	Reserved Books
Principles of Economics	Term Paper	Periodicals
English Literature	Nonterm Paper	General Collection
Community and Personal Hygiene	Nonterm Paper	Periodicals
Introduction to Philosophy	Term Paper	General Collection
Introduction to Government	Term Paper	General Collection
General Psychology	Term Paper	General Collection
Introduction to Sociology	Term Paper	General Collection
Geography	Nonterm Paper	Atlases
Speech	Oral Classwork	General Collection
Geology	Background Information	Reserve Periodical

Table 11 clearly reveals that, as previous studies have shown, the *term paper* impels students to use the resources of the library-media center above all other impellers. Like previous studies of two-year colleges the general collection best fills this need. It is noteworthy that of the 347 different courses offered only 17 were responsible for generating 20 or more withdrawals on an accumulative basis over the four one-week sampling periods by the four two-year colleges who participated in this portion of the investigation.

Table 12 reveals that only in one college each were art, business, drama, engineering and health and physical education library-dependent. There were four colleges in which there were two courses each sufficiently library-dependent to generate ten percent of the library-media withdrawals during the four sampling periods; they were: physical sciences, psychology, social science, speech. History was L-MC dependent in four colleges. Leading all courses was English which was L-MC dependent in five out of the seven two-year colleges investigated.

The results shown in Table 13 suggest that with the possible exception of English and history, the use of library-media materials is more dependent upon the instructor as an impeller than upon the nature of the course. These results are consistent with the findings reported in *Teaching and the Community College Library.*

Table 13 again clearly reveals how powerful the term paper is as an assignment to generate the use of the resources of the library-media center. Little dependence on the center results from the assignment of lab reports, class discussion, speech tests or play production. The one encouraging impeller of L-MC withdrawals is shown by the relatively large number of withdrawals for background information.

It is noteworthy, as Table 14 shows, that not only are withdrawals from the general collection over five times greater than from the reserve collection, but that periodicals were withdrawn at a rate nearly 50 percent greater than for withdrawals from the reserve collection. This pattern of withdrawals is nearly reversed in comparison with studies reported in Patricia B. Knapp's *College Teaching and the College Library,* p. 59. According to Knapp, four-year colleges and universities were noted for the greater use by their students of the reserve collection than of the general or periodical collection—a contrast to results revealed by studies of the two-year college. Indeed, Table 14 shows, without exception, that greater reliance was placed by instructors and students on the general collection than on any other portion of the collection in all seven two-year colleges in the study.

TABLE 12

COURSES WHICH ACCOUNTED FOR 10 PERCENT OR MORE LIBRARY WITHDRAWALS IN ONE OR MORE OF SEVEN TWO-YEAR COLLEGES DURING FOUR SAMPLING PERIODS

College	Art	Business	Drama	Engineering	English	Health & Phys. Ed	History	Physical Sciences	Psychology	Social Sciences	Speech
A	2.87	–	11.49	1.72	24.80	6.89	18.96	–	2.28	–	10.34
B	15.06	11.65	–	21.01	4.66	–	.63	10.81	.84	6.99	.21
C	4.44	.27	.15	.02	26.76	8.64	9.02	2.78	6.49	1.52	14.65
D	–	–	–	–	30.40	.52	2.63	12.62	12.01	15.02	–
E	6.09	–	–	1.67	29.47	–	22.33	–	2.32	21.86	8.83
F	.48	–	–	4.32	34.18	–	12.50	4.32	4.32	8.64	5.28
G	–	–	–	4.65	6.97	32.55	23.25	–	32.55	4.65	–

TABLE 13

MAIN COURSE PURPOSE OF LIBRARY WITHDRAWALS IN SEVEN TWO-YEAR COLLEGES

College	Term Paper	Paper— Not Term	Lab Report	Class Discussion	Oral Classwork	Test— Not Speech	Test— Speech	Play Production	Background Info.	Other
A	14	4	0	0	2	0	0	0	6	11
B	53	12	10	9	5	5	1	2	35	35
C	218	181	40	42	100	110	2	1	169	143
D	30	32	21	4	22	63	0	9	8	20
E	7	3	1	3	2	11	0	1	3	9
F	28	3	1	0	1	5	0	0	0	3
G	4	9	1	1	1	9	1	0	5	0
Totals	354	244	74	59	133	203	4	13	226	221

TABLE 14

TYPES AND NUMBERS OF LIBRARY WITHDRAWALS IN SEVEN TWO-YEAR COLLEGES
DURING FOUR SAMPLING PERIODS

College	General Collection	Reserve Books	Periodicals	Reserve Periodicals	Textbook	Pamphlet	College Catalog	Other
A	24	2	4	0	0	12	6	2
B	152	13	16	1	48	8	1	9
C	297	76	168	61	75	21	2	85
D	188	28	15	23	3	0	13	6
E	34	18	2	1	1	0	0	1
F	39	5	5	4	4	1	1	2
G	30	2	0	2	0	0	0	1
Totals	764	144	210	92	131	42	23	106

Perhaps the most interesting statistic revealed in Table 14 is the importance students placed on the withdrawal of textbooks. At first blush, this may seem strange, but many students who attend a two-year college come from economic environments less favorable than those who attend four-year colleges and universities. Thus, for some students, the possibility of having textbooks in the library-media center for their use can save them valuable dollars which might otherwise preclude attendance or make it extremely difficult to attend college at all. It would be well for two-year college L-MC's to carefully examine their purchasing policy with respect to textbooks. It would seem from the *Seven-College Study* reported on these pages that the allocation of a small percentage of the L-MC budget for the purchase of textbooks would be one of the most realistic and meaningful expenditures that the two-year college library-media center can make.

Table 15 would seem to suggest that freshman students in two-year colleges are more heavy borrowers of library media materials than sophomore students. This is not true, however, since typically students with sophomore standing represent but one-third of the total enrollment at a two-year college. With this factor kept in mind, it can be clearly seen that *percentage-wise* the sophomore student is a considerably heavier borrower of materials from the library-media center than freshman students. The same holds true of female students. Female students typically make up a little more than one-third of the enrollment in two-year colleges, yet it can be seen, notwithstanding this fact, more withdrawals were made by female than by male students. The results shown in Table 15 have been borne out by studies previously cited in this chapter as well as others.

Student Use of L-MC Materials and Teaching Effectiveness. In two of the colleges in the Seven College Study there was a competent administrator who agreed to evaluate the teaching effectiveness of his staff independent of any knowledge as to how many L-MC withdrawals the students of each instructor made. The investigator correlated these teaching evaluations with the withdrawal purposes reported by the students during the four spaced one-week sampling periods. These results are reported in Tables 16 and 17.

It will be noted in Table 16 that the personal evaluations by the administrators clearly reveal a statistically significant correlation between those ranked in the upper one-third in teaching effectiveness as compared to those evaluated in the lower one-third as associated with the use of library-media materials. Thus, these findings, confirming the re-

TABLE 15

LIBRARY WITHDRAWALS BY CLASS STANDING AND SEX FROM SEVEN TWO-YEAR COLLEGES DURING FOUR ONE-WEEK SAMPLING PERIODS

College	Freshman Male	Freshman Female	Sophomore Male	Sophomore Female	Freshman Totals	Sophomore Totals
A	8	12	13	17	20	30
B	76	90	60	32	166	92
C	371	476	470	421	847	891
D	69	66	67	65	135	132
E	21	13	13	11	34	24
F	7	20	18	17	27	35
G	12	8	8	7	20	15
Totals	564	685	649	570	1249	1219

TABLE 16

RATED TEACHING EFFECTIVENESS AS ASSOCIATED WITH STUDENT USE OF LMC MATERIALS AT TWO TWO-YEAR COLLEGES

College	Lower Ranked Third			Middle Ranked Third			Upper Ranked Third		
	No. of Teachers	No. of Withdrawals	Av. Withdrawal Per Teacher	No. of Teachers	No. of Withdrawals	Av. Withdrawal Per Teacher	No. of Teachers	No. of Withdrawals	Av. Withdrawal Per Teacher
A	4	1	0.25	20	44	2.20	13	104	8.00
B	108	675	6.25	94	1254	13.34	82	859	10.47
	112	676	6.03	114	1298	11.38	95	963	10.13

TABLE 17

RATED TEACHING EFFECTIVENESS AS ASSOCIATED WITH STUDENT USE OF LIBRARY MATERIALS IN ENGLISH, HISTORY AND SOCIAL SCIENCE CLASSES AT TWO TWO-YEAR COLLEGES

College	Lower Ranked Third			Middle Ranked Third			Upper Ranked Third		
	No. of Teachers	No. of Withdrawals	Av. Withdrawal per Teacher	No. of Teachers	No. of Withdrawals	Av. Withdrawal per Teacher	No. of Teachers	No. of Withdrawals	Av. Withdrawal per Teacher
A	2	1	0.50	5	30	6.00	4	27	6.75
B	33	403	12.21	30	578	19.26	23	454	19.73
Average	35	404	11.57	35	608	17.37	27	481	17.81

sult reported in the previous chapter on secondary education, strongly
suggests that the more effective teachers impel students to use the resources of the L-MC than those adjudged less competent in teaching
effectiveness. The results are similarly conclusive between those faculty
ranked in the lower one-third in teaching effectiveness as compared to
those ranked in the middle one-third. There, however, is less conclusive
evidence between the middle and upper third ranked instructors with
respect to teaching effectiveness as associated with student use of library-
media materials.

Table 17 perhaps is even more meaningful and significant than the results revealed by Table 16. In Table 16 all the faculty are included for
each college even though research has revealed that the departments of
English, History, and Social Sciences together account for close to 85
percent of all withdrawals from an L-MC.

Table 17 reveals, without exception, that those areas in a college which
traditionally make the greatest demand upon the L-MC collection dis-
criminates at all three levels with respect to teaching effectiveness as
associated with student use of the center's collection. That is to say,
the students of those faculty administratively rated in the upper one-
third of the teaching staff withdrew more materials than the middle one-
third and those in the middle one-third withdrew more materials than
the lower one-third.

The results shown in Tables 16 and 17, like the similar results reported
in the previous chapter in one high school, must, of course, be cautiously
interpreted inasmuch as these have been the only known studies conducted to date on the relationship of teaching effectiveness to L-MC
usage. Moreover, it must be remembered that the evaluation results were
based upon a single, albeit knowledgeable, administrator in each institution. It would be interesting to know if similar results would be obtained
by peer group evaluation and student evaluation. The investigator
hypothesizes that similar results would occur.

Conclusions: the L-MC User and Non-user

From these various studies it can be concluded that the L-MC user is
more likely to be a female than a male student. The L-MC user is especially likely to pick up a library card as early as possible; to withdraw
books from the general collection; to spend much time in the L-MC and
to have a native curiosity which prompts reading for personal pleasure
as well as for courses taken. This student has enjoyed reading ever since
childhood, and has an innate love of books fostered by parental encourage-

ment. Coming from a higher socioeconomic stratum than the nonuser, the L-MC user works less hours per week for pay, and lives in the family home which contains many books, including a fairly substantial collection of paperbacks which the student has bought. Seldom indulging in light, nonthought-provoking publications, this student's reading tastes run to the controversial, so that both personal and course reading are taken up with ideas. These furnish the basis for discussion both in class and among friends—which the student enjoys. Next to meeting the requirements for term papers and speeches (the chief techniques by which instructors impel use of the L-MC in a course-related sense), the L-MC user searches the L-MC for background material which will permit intelligent participation in class and/or group discussion.

Compared to the nonuser, the user is younger; has greater scholastic aptitude; repeats in college the higher scholastic achievement attained in high school; carries more units each semester, but has completed fewer college units over all. The L-MC user is likely taking a course or courses in art history; English and speech; introduction to music; electronic circuitry; health or introduction to health, physical education, and recreation; geology; Western civilization or United States history; introduction to philosophy or religions of the world; introduction to government, general psychology, or introductory sociology. Without a college L-MC, this student would feel denied a very important part of the educational process as a whole.

The L-MC nonuser in two-year colleges is more likely to be a male than a female student, and probably is slightly older than the mean of the student body *in toto*. He is more likely to be living away from home than with his family. He is somewhat less able than the student body as a whole in the following respects: scholastic aptitude; scholastic achievement in high school; and scholastic record in college. Based upon his father's occupation, the L-MC nonuser's socioeconomic stratum is lower than the average for the student body, although he works for pay only about one half-hour per week longer than the student population as a whole. He carries fewer units each semester, but has completed more units on a cumulative basis. Though he buys paperbacks and saves his textbooks, using these sources as references for his course work, his home library is sparser than that of the L-MC user. The L-MC nonuser does not wish to be "bothered" with checking library materials in and out; nor, since he is forgetful, does he want the annoyance of receiving overdue notices. In consequence, he never picks up a library card, being inclined to use the L-MC chiefly as a place to study out of a textbook.

He is likely to be taking courses in agriculture, business, engineering, fire science, foreign languages, mathematics and police science. But if a term paper is not assigned in any of these courses, he makes little, if any, use of the L-MC except, possibly, for doing homework out of a textbook.

The "profiles" outlined above describe the personal characteristics of the L-MC user and nonuser at a typical two-year college.

Implementation of procedures to facilitate greater usage of L-MC materials, other than the assignment of term papers and speeches, would suggest instructional approaches, as was reported earlier, which are issue oriented or require problem solving. Other effective L-MC usage impelling means would be the implementation of certain aspects of English primary school education. Still another effective means for facilitating meaningful usage of the interdisciplinary resources housed in the L-MC would be the use of performance based contract learning. Still further means for facilitating meaningful usage of the resources of the L-MC is the implementation of imaginative L-MC practices. The remainder of this chapter will focus on some of these successful practices.

Survey of Forty Leading L-MCs

In 1972, under the auspices of the American Association of Junior Colleges, Max R. Raines, Professor of Higher Education at Michigan State University, conducted a survey to identify current practices and trends in community services and other programs by leading L-MCs.

More than 1,000 post cards were sent out soliciting nominations of outstanding L-MCs. Two hundred thirty-two two-year colleges were nominated. Fifty-three L-MCs were mentioned 3 or more times, the median number of mentioned times of these 53 was 5, and the range was from 3-25 nominations. A questionnaire was sent to each of these 53 colleges. Responses to the questionnaire were received from 41 colleges; however only 40 arrived in time for analysis.

The Sample

The estimated population of the areas served by responding colleges ranged from the 3,000 served by Louisburg Community College to 1.5 million in the district of the El Centro Campus of Dallas County Junior College. Student enrollment data, reported for fall, 1971, reflected a proportionately wide range. Full-time student enrollment totals ranged from 556 at Mississippi Gulf Coast to 9,563 at Nassau Community College in Garden City, New York. The average full-time student enroll-

ment for the 39 responding colleges was 3,700. Mississippi Gulf Coast
College reported the lowest part-time student enrollment (19) while
Orange Coast College reported the largest part-time enrollment (13,634).

The data submitted on numbers of faculty and L-MC staff members
showed variations similar to those described above. Full-time faculty
totals range from 41 (Coffeyville Community College) to 382 (Central
Piedmont Community College). Central Piedmont which ranks approximately eighth in full-time enrollment of the 40 reporting colleges, reported the highest totals in areas of full-time faculty and full-time professional L-MC staff.

Para-professionals are employed on a full-time basis by 22 of the 40
reporting colleges and on a part-time basis by seven colleges. All but
four colleges employ technically skilled staff on a full-time and/or part-
time basis. While the average number of full-time technical staff is 6.6,
it should be noted that two institutions, Golden West College and
Brookdale Community College, employ 24 and 30 full-time technical
staff respectively. In the case of both Golden West and Brookdale,
technical staff serve a major role in the implementation of comprehensive college-wide AVT programs.

Analysis of Response Patterns to the Structured Questions

Integration of Library and Learning Resource Center. It seemed desirable to determine the extent to which the reporting colleges had integrated their libraries and learning resource centers. Table 18 shows
that there is a predominate practice of integrating the library and learning resources center, and that trend seems likely to continue in the years
ahead.

Extent of Service to Various Constituencies. Community colleges have
become increasingly aware of the need to serve a broader range of constituencies. This awareness has stemmed largely from the social revolution.
Table 19 shows the extent to which the impact has been experienced
within library and learning resource centers.

Table 19 reflects the current level of response as well as the response
anticipated by 1976. Examination of the table demonstrates a model
pattern which indicates that the L-MCs *willingly assist* any group which
seeks assistance and expect to continue to do so in the coming years.
To identify the extent to which services may be expanded one needs to
consider the level of responses to *actively cultivate* and *no need identified.*
Here we see that at least one fourth of the respondents perceive no cur-

TABLE 18

EXTENT OF INTEGRATION OF LIBRARY AND LEARNING
RESOURCES CENTER IN RESPONDING
COMMUNITY COLLEGES

Operational Area	Currently				By 1976			
	Entirely Separate	More Separate Than Integrated	More Integrated Than Separate	Entirely Integrated	Entirely Separate	More Separate Than Integrated	More Integrated Than Separate	Entirely Separate
Central Purposes	2	3	7	28	1	2	6	31
Budget	6	6	3	27	2	4	6	29
Direct Administrative Supervision	4	2	3	31	2	1	6	32
College Division Assignment	4	2	3	30	2	1	5	30
Operating Staff	6	4	6	25	2	1	10	28

rent need to serve elementary students and faculty, parochial students and faculty, and labor union officials.

By 1976, more than one fourth of the respondents anticipate *active cultivation* of high school students and faculty as well as hospital staffs, social agency personnel, senior citizens and ethnic minorities. In fact almost half of the respondents anticipate *active cultivation* of hospital

TABLE 19

EXTENT OF SERVICE TO VARIOUS CONSTITUENCIES

Constituencies	Currently			By 1976		
	We Actively Cultivate	We Willingly Assist	No Need Identified	We Actively Cultivate	We Willingly Assist	No Need Identified
A. Area Public Schools						
High School Students	4	33	3	8*	18	1
High School Faculty	2	33	4	9*	16	3
Elementary Students	0	16	24**	2	13	11*
Elementary Faculty	0	34	16*	5	18	6
B. Parochial Schools						
Students	1	21	17*	3	16	7
Faculty	0	25	13*	3	17	5
C. University Extension Centers						
Students	2	25	11*	5	17	6
Faculty	1	24	12	4	16	7*
D. Local Community						
Hospital Staffs	9	23	8	11*	13	5
Elected Civic Leaders	2	33	5	6	19	5
Gov. Agency Personnel	2	30	8	6	20	4
Social Agency Personnel	2	31	6	8*	16	5
Business Leaders	2	31	6	7	17	4
Labor Union Officials	1	21	18*	5	13	11*
Senior Citizens	4	27	8	9*	15	5
Ethnic Minorities	8	27	5	14*	12	4
Other	5	16	5	4	11	5

*Represents at least one fourth of the respondents to that particular item.
**Represents more than half of the respondents to that particular item.

staffs and ethnic minority groups. Only three groups are viewed as having *no need* by more than one quarter of the respondents. They were as follows: elementary students, university extension faculty and labor union officials. (The non-involvement and anticipation of *no need* among labor union officials leads one to wonder if either a middle class bias is operating or if there is uneasiness about reaction from the Boards of Trustees if labor union officials were to be served.)

Territorial Tensions. The AAJC advisory group suggested that one constraint on expansion of community services might be found in the tensions it would create with other libraries in the service area. It is quite apparent that organizational conflicts arise rapidly when operational territories are perceived as being invaded. Table 20 indicates that the vast majority of the respondents in this study have not encountered tension of any consequence. It seems safe to say, whether they will en-

TABLE 20

TERRITORIAL TENSION OR CONFLICT

	Considerable Tension	Some Tension	No Tension	Not Applicable for Us
Public Library (city)	2	4	24	4
Public Library (county)	2	4	23	10
School Libraries	0	3	32	3
University Libraries	0	2	27	10
State Libraries	1	1	24	11
Other (please list)	0	0	8	5
Research Libraries	0	1	22	12
Law, Religious, etc.	0	0	1	0

counter conflict in the future depends on the extent to which they expand services without establishing cooperative arrangements with other libraries in the area—particularly public libraries.

Informational Resource Role. There also was a concern with the current and anticipated role which the L-MC might assume in relationships to providing informational resources to local government officials. It was assumed that as a major resource center in the community the L-MC might be in an excellent position to assist or even press for use of available knowledge and information in the decision-making processes of the community.

To ascertain the role Professor Raines attempted to define a series of sequential postures that might be taken in this regard. Table 21 reflects a possible trend in this direction as one examines both the responses to each item as well as the cumulative responses. By scoring this rating scale from 1 to 6 we find that currently the average rating is 2.5 and the average rating increases to 3.2 for the 1976 response patterns. Said another way, while only 2 respondents (5%) currently see their programs (a) maintaining telephone liaison with various community officials; (b) providing bibliographies and abstracting services to them; and (c) providing reproductions of key articles and documents, almost 13 respondents (33%) of them anticipate achieving that level or greater by 1976. It appears we may anticipate greater emphasis and concern for the information resource role in the years ahead.

Summary. The major impression from the "hard data" is that the commitment to community involvement is generally limited at this time. There does appear to be an emerging awareness of possible need for such service. It is too early to determine if there is any definite trend in that direction. Neither the instrumentation used in this study nor the response pattern warrant such a conclusion. The following part of the report does include some interesting and promising practices which might entice some L-MCs to explore and expand their community involvements.

Summaries of Promising Practices in Community Services for L-MCs

The requests for descriptions of programs and activities were divided into eight areas. They are defined and the number of descriptions* received for each area are listed as follows:

1. *Cross-Cultural.* Any program which L-MCs develop or contribute to in developing cross-cultural understanding through art exhibits, dis-

---

*An attempt was made to differentiate programs from activities but the effort did not communicate well to respondents; consequently, both are included in this report.

TABLE 21

INFORMATIONAL RESOURCE PROGRAM

Local governmental officials, agency personnel, and other civic leaders are faced with complex decisions and often have a minimum of relevant, reliable information on which to base their decisions. Some authorities feel that libraries must develop information research programs to alleviate this condition. Others feel that the community college library has its hands full just meeting the needs of its own faculty and student body. To sort out the positions on this matter, we have constructed a series of operational practices.

By 1976	Σ	Now	Σ	Statement
1	1	2	2	We routinely refer all requests coming from outside our faculty and student body because community services has not been accepted as part of the LIB/LRC role
14	15	18	20	We gladly accept external requests and help when possible, but usually have to refer many requests to more comprehensive libraries
12	27	18	38	We are sufficiently comprehensive to meet most of the current requests received from the community leadership constituency.
9	36	1	39	We not only are able to meet most requests but also have appointed a college staff member to maintain a continuing telephone liaison with various community officials and leaders to provide resources such as bibliographic and abstracting services, census tracts, reproduction of key articles, important public documents, community archives, personnel directories of resource persons, etc.
2	38	1	40	In addition to last statement above we have assigned several staff members (including faculty) who regularly visit with community leaders to ascertain their informational and resource needs and to design necessary packages of information for distribution.
2	40	0	40	We have implemented the last two statements and also prepare news releases about those public officials and agencies who are making a genuine effort to obtain and use relevant and reliable information in their decision-making.

plays of cultural artifacts and crafts, ethnic musical presentations, dance programs, etc. 12 responses

2. *Career Information.* Any program designed to establish career information systems on a community-wide basis through cooperative efforts with area counselors, employment security commissions, public schools, social agencies, and manpower commissions. 11 responses

3. *Community Information Systems.* Any program designed to collect, codify, and package information pertaining to needs, problems, and resources of the community; to establish mechanisms for delivering the information to citizens and community leaders; and to identify resource personnel in the community to serve in advisory capacities to a variety of community groups (e.g. youth groups, recreation programs, drug centers, city planning, commissions, model cities). 5 responses

4. *Community Issues Program.* Any program designed to collect and organize materials around the central and critical issues of the community and to develop ways of encouraging use of such information (issues centers, forums, discussion groups, bibliographies, etc.). 8 responses

5. *Learning Resource Packaging.* Any programs designed to produce and distribute learning resource packages for citizens enrolled in nontraditional study programs; for community agencies which sponsor educationally related workshops, conferences, minorities, adult women, low-income adults, physically handicapped, educationally disadvantaged, institutionalized persons, etc.) 7 responses

6. *Inter-Agency Information Exchange.* Any programs designed to assist community agencies, organizations, and institutions in becoming aware of the functions, programs, membership, range and schedule of activities of other related organizations within the community. 4 responses

7. *Leisure-Time Activity.* Any programs designed to assist community agencies, organizations, and institutions in becoming aware of the functions, programs, membership, range and schedule of activities of other related organizations within the community. 5 responses

8. *Other.* Any programs that did not fit into the preceding categories. 5 responses

The 67 descriptions came from a core of 19 separate colleges. The range in number of descriptions of programs was from 1 to 8 with median of 2 for the institutions providing descriptions. It was apparent that about a half a dozen L-MCs are moving into a *relatively* sophisticated level of community services programming.

Cross-Cultural Programming. At Wharton Junior College in Texas the fine arts division and the learning center have cooperated with several approaches in promoting cross-cultural programs. Art students of the month are recognized with special exhibits. Class work including sculpture, crafts, sketching, etc., are of special interest. Traveling exhibits have been selected by the art department. Students from other countries are encouraged to exhibit items which are indicative of the culture of their countries. During special weeks, such as the Negro History week, films are shown, book reviews are presented and media exhibits are arranged. Most exhibits can be displayed without any charge. The respondent reports that the only problem seems to be time. "If one only had time to follow through on these exhibits with program calendars, bibliographies, and research for other resources of information." The students are very pleased with their own involvement in these programs. The community participates in items of current interest, and a portion of the community attends the art displays (one of the greatest successes was the elementary art display sponsored by the Fine Arts Division).

San Antonio College in Texas sponsors a three-week exhibit of minority art to afford students an opportunity to relate to barrio art. A display of art from the barrios was assembled by MECHA and open to students and community visitors. The response was good and the college felt the outcome satisfactory.

Shoreline Community College in Washington and Lansing Community College in Michigan have also featured artwork and artifacts of minorities and other cultures. The duration of these exhibits is intermittent, and there is no cost to the library.

The respondent from Lane Community College in Oregon indicated that a small museum is really needed to do a proper job but until then the library had displays of artifacts and crafts and recorded ethnic music. The purpose is to acquaint the students with cultural heritage and crafts of Northwest Indian cultures. The exhibit is open to the college students and the public during the hours the library is open. They now have a $16,000 collection on indefinite loan to the college. Ethnic music is available on the information retrieval system through FM listening. The program is operated without need for additional personnel. Response has been very good.

The Northern Virginia Community College central campus library offers on-going art exhibits all year round. The art exhibits are one man shows, student displays, and local art cultural association exhibits. Special awards and prizes are made, and receptions held in the L-MC facility. Support

for these programs are provided by audio-visual services in supplying
lecturns, microphones, speakers, and taped background music. Displays are routinely made in several display areas of student exhibits,
faculty publications, and items of local and national interest. Eastern
Campus L-MC actively supports campus cultural programs, despite lack
of space in current temporary quarters. Student art work is continuously
displayed. The L-MC was used for displays during National Negro History
week, Spring 1971. The Fine Arts festival for 1972 concluded with a
music festival held in the L-MC.

Career Information. With the mounting career crisis in this country
there is an increasing emphasis on career related programs in community
colleges. The investigator and advisory committee, therefore, were eager
to learn of the career information activities among the leading L-MCs.
Several programs of note were identified.

A computer based occupational information data bank is in operation
at Lane Community College in Oregon. This is to provide high school
and college students with up-to-date data on career opportunities, requirements, and compensation—cooperative programs with public
schools, state employment offices, counselors, social agencies, voca-
tional-rehabilitation agencies, welfare agencies, etc. Counselors and the
librarian are the staff supporters. The cost to the college is for the rental
of the computer terminal which interrogates the computer. Audio
cassettes also are available for detailed information within job clusters
and are immediately available to the students. The program has been
expanded to include high schools throughout the intermediate education district. Response has been very positive and helpful to students.
The problems have been minimal.

The Learning Resources Laboratory at North Florida Junior College
has furnished personnel to present audio-visual programs to schools in
the area and to the various civic clubs. Filmstrips and records on career
information are provided for students on campus and for interested
citizens. Slide programs have been made to be presented to high school
students in the field of vocational education (auto-mechanics, nursing,
cosmetology).

Golden West College utilizes a systems approach to implement their
guidance philosophy and procedures, including career information.
They provided an interesting and well-conceived plan that has been im-
plemented by the guidance department with assistance from the L-MC

in developing material. In a summary comment the Golden West respondent said "Our efforts are aimed at providing our staff, students, and prospective students with a system of guidance activity which will allow the individual to obtain the necessary information at the appropriate time. We do not feel that a career guidance center as a separate unit will be functional in a community college." Golden West has emphasized that occupational/educational information as well as assistance with "self" identification in implementing realistic goals must be an integral part of the student's total college experience—not tucked away in one room or occurring at one time.

Bellevue Community College in Washington has a workshop for prospective small business owners and/or managers in the local area. The cost is minimal for this one day workshop operated by one librarian from his institution, and a prominent local businessman. A bibliography of sources and resources is prepared, and this program has been well received.

The purpose of the career information services at Chabot College Library is to assist local community agencies with immediate support for presentation in local career days, with emphasis on special programs such as library technology, and photography. Contacts are made with area counselors, public schools, business and governmental agencies concerning career information and recruitment. The L-MC also participates in retraining activities, through closed circuit television, dealing with group agencies such as police and fire departments. Instructional resources used are television, audio-visual equipment and materials with L-MC personnel acting as resource consultants in the development of techniques and materials for retraining. The L-MC also supports and assists in two community programs, sponsored by other institutions, for the development of career information and career retraining in nursing and medical terminology.

Community Information Systems. Bellevue Community College in Washington offers a legislative reference service to keep students, faculty, and the community informed of the latest action (and the action to date) of the state legislature concerning legislation affecting community colleges, in particular, and affecting education, in general. This is handled by presently employed reference librarians. They pull together the latest legislative information, current status of bills, bills passed, etc. and make them available in the L-MC for use by students, faculty and community.

In addition, the latest legislative news is made available over CHESTER, the dial-access retrieval system at Bellevue and can be retrieved by people in the community (as well as throughout the state and union) on a 24-hour basis, seven days a week.

Chabot College in California has in their L-MC a number of programs involved in collecting and codifying information for the use of the community. The L-MC tries to keep informed as to community needs. They have developed a vertical file of community information along with a newspaper clipping file for use by people in the community. The L-MC has also cooperated with community agencies in the preparation of video tape to be played back by local cable TV systems.

Community Issues Programs. The primary concern of Central Piedmont Community College in Charlotte, North Carolina is creating a more politically aware campus. They had a 27″ x 34″ flip chart that covers current political primaries of local, state, and national concern. This was mounted in the front area of the L-MC near the circulation desk. Its purpose was to keep students and faculty informed as to the positions of the candidates of all the parties. The Head of Circulation handled all the posting of clippings from newspapers and magazines and all the exhibits. This program lasted through the local May primaries and was reactivated during late summer at the time of national conventions and through the November elections.

Fullerton Junior College in California provides facilities for a Center for the Study of the Future of Man which contains L-MC materials as well as materials belonging to members of interested community groups. The room is serving as a center for studies on environment, pollution, ecology. High school students in the community are invited to use the room in their environmental studies.

Two continuing education programs at Golden West College are worthy of mention. They are the annual "Congress for Community Progress," a joint venture of the Huntington Beach Chamber of Commerce and the American Management Association; and community related "Explorations in Communication," sponsored wholly by Golden West College and designed to bridge the generation gap, to bring students, staff, and citizens together in open and conversant dialogue. The "Congress for Community Progress" is attended by selected community leaders. It lasts for one day each year with 150 to 250 participants. Activities consisting of forums, films, seminars and guest speakers are provided and

local citizens also serve as consultants and discussion leaders. The costs
are borne by the Chamber of Commerce/American Management Association. One of the problems encountered has been the need for continuing evaluation, and another problem has been publicity. It is hoped that
a better understanding of problems faced by the burgeoning community
may be gained through this program. "Explorations in Communication"
is open to anyone wishing to participate. It lasts for six weeks and there
are six three-hour sessions. There are about 4-6 groups which consist of
less than 25 members per group. These open discussion groups are staffed
by faculty, staff, and students. The cost is absorbed by a small staff budget.

At Lane Community College the college telecasting students have a
half hour news broadcast of events which they believe the college and
community should be made aware. These may be issues involving services
the college has to offer, problems of student unrest, ecological questions
related to the local area, or the dismissal of a staff member. The telecasts
are objective and straightforward in their approach. Any viewer may see
these telecasts on the two major network stations in the area or they
may have access to them through the dial access information retrieval
system. The college has had an excellent response from the general public and the students. The cost is about $5,000 per year for film and tape.

Special card bibliographies on Ethnic Studies: Chicano, Black, and
Indian are available at Lane Community College in Oregon. There also
is a card bibliography on Environmental Issues. Eugene Register Guard
index (no other institution produces an index to the principal newspaper
of the area), and information files on local issues is maintained by the
college. All of these prgorams are designed to make information more
easily retrieved. Anyone who finds the LCC L-MC accessible may use it
and no extra staff has been required.

Learning Resource Packaging. Lane Community College has consumer
packages for homemakers (at home), buying guides, menu planning guides,
sewing guides, and games for rainy days. For blind students they have
books in braille and textbooks on tape, 450 cassette tape recorders, and
6,000 cassettes in many fields including math, science, language arts,
and foreign languages. Programs designated "outreach" are open entry/
exit in design and include math and business courses. They are used in
areas of their district as much as 30 to 70 miles away. Several programs
were cooperative efforts with other institutions to achieve better articu-

lation. VIP (Vocational Instructional Packages) include about 850
packets covering many areas—auto diesel, machine technology, industrial technology, drafting, welding, nursing, and others. Another cooperative program is ICE (Independent Curriculum for Electronics) with 156
packages—a comprehensive program in basic electronics.

Physically and mentally handicapped adults from Interlake Manor
(State Department of Institutions) and Eastside Handicappers (Sheltered
Workshop) are served with Learning Resources Packaging at Bellevue
Community College. This includes students with cerebral palsy who are
in wheelchairs, some of whom are nonverbal. Also included are some
mentally retarded who are not physically handicapped. The Library
Media Center and the Individual Development Opportunity Center cooperate on this program and share a full-time professional librarian who
has background experience in this area. Activities include library orientation on an individual basis, the use of film loops and film strips in the
AVT learning lab, the use of 8 mm and 16 mm films, both for handicapped people on the campus and those to whom they take the service
at Interlake Manor. Also included is the use of the dial-access information retrieval system housed in the L-MC. The system permits off-campus
calls on a 24-hour, 7 day per week basis. One dial-access carrel in the
L-MC is adapted with special equipment so that it can be operated by students with cerebral palsy; just one finger is needed to activate the "touch
tone" buttons on the control panel. Moreover, library service is provided
on an individualized basis for handicapped students of varying reading
abilities, both on campus and at Interlake Manor. The service to Interlake
Manor involves patrons who presently are not receiving any other library
service from the community.

Bellevue Community College in Washington has the help of CHESTER.
CHESTER, a Dial-Access Information Retrieval System (DAIRS), is designed to help meet the learning needs of students, the instructional
needs of faculty, and the informational needs of the community. Students, faculty and community members participate. The programming
of CHESTER is handled by a media specialist, and assisted by a part-
time student assistant. Technical problems and the maintenance and
servicing of the system are handled by a full-time technician and his
assistant, who maintain, repair, and service all of the audio-visual systems
and equipment on campus. Audio and video lessons, lectures, legislative
information, current events, and other audio-visual taped and filmed
materials are programmed on the system on a weekly basis. The dial-

access system is reprogrammed each week-end in order to keep the information up-to-date and of interest to the users. The weekly schedule is published and the scheduled programs are available to students, faculty, and community users on a 24-hour basis 7 days per week. The response has been overwhelming. More than 2,000 off-campus calls are received per week, in addition to the tremendous usage on campus. At the present time, only community users with touch-tone telephones can select programs to listen to. The college has touch-tone telephones (connected with tele-lecture units) to permit students and faculty (as well as the people in those communities) to "access" programs on CHESTER, to listen individually, or to make the programs available to larger groups by tying in with the tele-lecture unit. Explorations are being made with the police and fire departments and with hospitals concerning the possibility of providing lectures, programmed lessons, and even credit courses through dial-access to meet the learning needs of persons employed in these community agencies.

The inmates at Bordentown Correctional Institution are benefiting from a program at Burlington County College at Pemberton, New Jersey to provide print resources for prisoners. Two paraprofessionals, who are paid under EEA funds, have developed a basic collection of books (reference and general) for the prison. A $13,000 matching grant was recently acquired to aid in furthering this program.

Inter-Agency Information Exchange. The Learning Resources Laboratory at North Florida Junior College served as a clearinghouse and a resource information center for the Madison Laubach Literacy Council whose purpose is to assist in finding tutors for illiterates and functional illiterates. The staff assists in locating materials for tutors. Two workshops have been held on campus to offer instruction to students and members of the community in the mechanics of tutoring. The Laubach Literacy Council gave permission for the Laboratory to tape their materials to be used outside the class. Resource Laboratory personnel can demonstrate the use of audiometers and vision testers to teachers in the area; and with this equipment they can identify candidates for referral to qualified specialists for hearing and seeing difficulties. Audio-visual programs have been provided for representatives of family services and of the Mental Health Association for the organization of a group of children of welfare recipients. The L-MC also provides inter-library loan services for business and professional members of the community.

Summary

It would appear that many promising ideas have emerged in recent years. While some require considerable expenditure of money, most of them are relatively modest in their requirements with respect to benefits received.

As should be evident from the reports, research findings, and studies described here, opportunities for challenging service in higher education are boundless. Knowledge of findings of such investigations as reported here can enable the library-media technologist to significantly aid in the teaching/learning process and thereby play a central role on the instructional team.

Finally, findings reported in this chapter can generally be considered as true and as applicable to four-year colleges and universities as to two-year colleges. The same broad generalization likely also holds true for secondary schools. That is, there is a commonality of *teaching procedures* and *L-MC practices* which seem to facilitate media usage and thereby learning.

THE COLLEGE AND UNIVERSITY LIBRARY

Librarians must be more than hat check girls in the halls of learning or a corps of ribbon clerks who are highly trained storekeepers of information—Anon

Because less integration of book and nonbook media exists in four-year colleges and universities as compared to school and two-year college L-MC's, more frequent use of the term "library" will be used in this chapter. Happily, an increasing number of each type of institution is moving toward a unified materials approach.

Four-year colleges and universities tend to have more individuality than the two-year college. Some are distinguished by their special programs such as a "junior year abroad." Some are distinguished by their teaching methodology. Some are distinguished by their experimental approach to education. Others are distinguished for a particular, strong, specialized academic interest.

There are in the United States more than one-thousand senior colleges and universities. They range in size from fewer than 500 students in the student body to more than 20,000. Because of the marked individuality with respect to programs mentioned above, there are few generalizations which can be aptly applied to this distinguished type of educational institution. Though the number of collegiate institutions has risen rapidly since our nation's founding, the growth of academic libraries attached to colleges and universities has been nothing short of phenomenal. There are at least a half dozen universities in the United States housing more than 3 million volumes. Universities housing 1 million or more volumes in their academic libraries throughout the world number in the hundreds.

The first academic library formed in the United States was not surprisingly attached to the first college—Harvard College. The collection began with 260 volumes given to it by John Harvard in 1638. These book gifts, added to by money gifts, resulted in the college being named for this Puritan minister benefactor. Today, Harvard College is Harvard

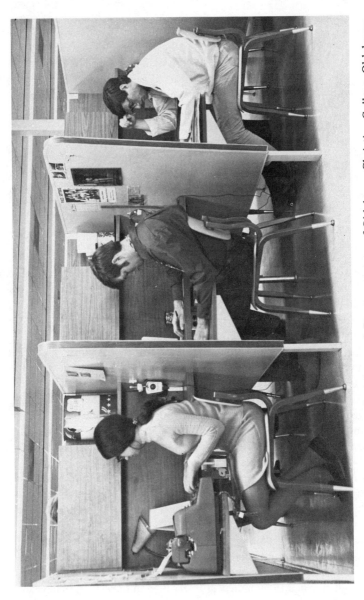

Each student has his own assigned study carrel. Photo courtesy of Oklahoma Christian College, Oklahoma City, Oklahoma.

University and the 260 original volumes have grown to nearly 8 million volumes. But the honor of having the first academic library on the North American continent does not belong to the United States but to Mexico. The University of Mexico, founded in 1551, today has nearly 100,000 students enrolled and with library resources in excess of 800,000 volumes.

The founding of Yale University like the founding of Harvard, was also connected with a gift of books to create a library for the new institution. But until the latter part of the 19th century academic libraries of the Harvards and Yales were small and usually contained only books associated with the restricted curricula of the period, predominately concerned with the education of men for the clergy. For more general works the students themselves, through their various debating, literary, and other undergraduate societies, created their own libraries. These reflected the students' interest in history, modern literature, politics, travel, and other subjects largely ignored in the official courses of instruction. In many instances these society libraries were larger and more varied than the central college library. As the literary societies were supplanted in the last half of the 19th century by the social fraternities, their libraries were often absorbed by the central library, leading to a great increase in the resources of the institution.

In the 20th century, academic libraries developed rapidly as instruments of teaching, as the textbook was increasingly supplemented by assigned sections of several books, to selections from books placed on reserve, to free research in the available literature. Long established university libraries today have large and diversified collections supporting all parts of the curriculum and, according to ALA statistics, about 5 percent of the university budget is allocated for maintenance of the collection.

Universities have developed great academic libraries to support the research to which they are devoted. Although the first university, Harvard, remains the nation's leader with its nearly 8 million volumes, it is noteworthy that in 1970 of the 50 largest university libraries with more than one million volumes each nearly two-thirds are state, rather than privately supported, institutions.

With the growth in the number of students, as well as the great size of many university libraries, many institutions have established separate undergraduate libraries, of which the Lamont Library (1948) at Harvard is perhaps the best known example. In addition to separate libraries for special schools, many colleges and universities have organized their collections around divisional reading rooms which provide the basic collections for broad academic disciplines. Increasingly, too, bookstacks are being opened so that students can have direct access to the collections.

Insofar as the demands placed on the resources of higher education are concerned, including libraries, it is noteworthy that the United States, with a smaller population, has three times as many students enrolled in its colleges and universities than all of Europe together. In toto, the United States in the fall of 1972 had 8.4 million students enrolled in postsecondary school education. This represents 39 students per 1,000 population. This compares with Sweden's 14 per 1,000 population (highest in Europe), England's 8, and West Germany's 5. As higher education enrollments soar to 12 million or more by the year 2000, according to projections made by the American Council on Education, it is obvious that ever greater demands will be placed upon the resources of libraries. This requires farsightedness and planning *before* the onslaught of eager learners arrive. However, with increasing attention focused on "university without walls" it may very well be that it will be the public community library, rather than the academic library, that will take the brunt of the onslaught.

Academic libraries form a group very similar throughout the world. They are descendants of the most ancient libraries. They cover a wide range of subjects in great detail to support the undergraduate students, the university's own instructors, and research workers. Many research libraries, moreover, attract scholars from all over the world. Though these libraries often benefit from outstanding gifts and bequests their main source of financial support comes from the college or university budget itself.

It is usual, insofar as acquisitions and the development of library policies are concerned, to have a standing Library Committee. Typically, each academic department is represented, with the Librarian serving as its chairman or secretary. In this way, acquisition balance is assured. Besides dependence on the Library Committee and faculty for acquisition recommendations, the Librarian and his staff use such selection tools as *Choice, American Libraries, College and Research Libraries*—indeed every reasonable source possible. Bibliographies, footnotes, television "book talk" shows, newspaper booklists such as *The New York Times Book Review,* magazines and journals such as *Saturday Review* and *Phi Delta*

Kappan are only some of the myriad resources used by alert modern day academic librarians. The media director and his staff use such selection tools as *Audiovisual Instruction* and *Educational Technology.*

The media director and his staff, like the library director and his staff, are responsible for the development of highly sophisticated services: ITV, C.A.I., dial access, and the like. Though there is some movement toward a "unified materials approach," and a similar unification of "library" and "media" staff on senior college and university campuses, this development has been slower than at most other types of educational institutions.

Research Findings

Harvey Branscomb, as he reported in *Teaching with Books* (1940), concluded from studies he conducted in student use of the library that the average student will withdraw twelve books per year from the general collection of his college or university. Almost two decades later a most comprehensive in-depth study of the role of the library in a four-year college was conducted by Patricia Knapp at Knox College, Illinois. The Knox College study, reported in *College Teaching and the College Library* (1959), corroborated most of Branscomb's findings.

Professor Knapp reported that 90 percent of the students made use of the library for course related purposes, that 40 percent of the courses accounted for 97 percent of the loans, and that about 45 percent of the student body were responsible for about 90 percent of the total loans made.

Psychology professor Gorham Lane, like library science professor Patricia Knapp, also made an impressive in-depth study of one institution—the University of Delaware. His contribution to the library research literature is unusual in one important respect, it was *longitudinal*—from the fall of 1961 to the winter of 1963. Moreover, Professor Lane's findings are notable for their implications to library-media technologists and other knowledge workers. His findings largely corroborated the research findings of Branscomb and Knapp. He found that students majoring in education, English, history, and political science made the greatest demand on the library collection. However, he found that not one of the five undergraduate schools at the University of Delaware impelled as many as 30 percent of its students to use the library for course related purposes.

It is interesting to note the similarities and dissimilarities in these library statistics reported for these senior collegiate institutions more than a decade ago as compared with reports made in a previous chapter with respect to the two-year colleges. In the College of the Desert study only 22.9 percent of the students entered the library for course related purposes, and in Kenneth Allen's study of three two-year Illinois colleges it was found that 49 percent of student entrants to their libraries were there for course related purposes as compared to 90 percent for Knox College students, but about the same as for the entrants at the University of Delaware. But one area of commonality throughout postsecondary collegiate education appears to be the rate of withdrawals of library-media materials. They tend to be similar in purpose within and between various types of institutions of higher education. Research results indicate that better than 80 percent of the actual loans made in two-year, four-year, and university libraries can be attributed to course related purposes. Research results also reveal that like the two-year college only a small percentage of the courses offered by senior colleges and universities are responsible for a large percentage of course withdrawals.

The economic effect of low utilization of library materials can be seen in a private eastern college which enrolled 2,300 full- and part-time students during 1965-66. There, 18,304 transactions occurred during the academic year which resulted in library salary costs of $1.54 per item circulated. Other prorated library costs to items circulated amounted to another $1.81. Total costs per item circulated thus came to $3.35. Though certainly no sweeping generalizations can be made from this single example nonetheless such figures along with other research results reported, certainly do suggest that library-media resources made available to students are not anywhere coming close to being fully utilized. If they were, the costs per loan would fall considerably below the transaction cost of $3.35 per loan. Yet, it can be remembered from the previous chapter that the total cost for each loan at College of the Desert was $4.58. It is self-evident that if these appallingly high transaction costs are to be reduced it must be through greater library impelling student assignments and/or through the reduction of the library budget itself.

During the 1965-66 academic year this writer investigated the relationship of circulation to costs and to F.T.E. [Full Time Equivalent (calculated by dividing the total number of semester hours taken by all enrolled students by 15)] students enrolled in representative universities of every geographical region of the country herein reported for the first time. Included among the universities investigated in the Hostrop Study were those considered to be the most prestigious in the land.

Table 22 reveals that the median number of loans of *all types* per F.T.E. student was 33.9—a figure substantially higher than that reported in most other previous studies which have largely reported only book loans from the general collection. Loans reported in Table 22 include both book and nonbook media. The figures as reported include periodicals and reserve books as well as books from the general collection. It is also noteworthy that the range of loans per F.T.E. student range from a low of 21.2 over a 12-month period to a high of 63.4.

It would be thought that University I which generated 93.7 loans per student would logically have among the lowest, if not the lowest dollar expenditure per loan. But this is not the case. In fact, of the nine universities reported in Table 22 its salary and nonsalary expenditures per loan ranked sixth most expensive.

Of further interest is the fact that the fewest loans per student did not correlate with the highest expenditure per student per loan. Indeed, University D, which generated the fewest loans per student (along with University G) had total expenditures per loan of $2.20 which ranked it a respectable fifth in terms of costs per loan.

It is extremely difficult to reconcile such a disparate range of loans per F.T.E. student. University I generated more than four times the number of loans as did Universities D and G. This wide difference may be accounted for as a result of one of several possibilities which further investigation may one day reveal. It may be the method used by various universities to record their circulation statistics and also what they consider to be circulation. It also may be attributed to the philosophy and policies of what can be circulated and where the circulated materials may be used: e.g., open stack systems versus closed stacks, the reserve collection vis-à-vis general collection, etc. It may be as one university reported that in its circulation count were any books, periodicals, etc. left lying on the library tables at the end of the day. Certainly, there appears to be more disparity than commonality among and between universities with respect to philosophy and method of recording circulation. University I, for example, which generated an astonishing 93.7 loans per F.T.E. students does not break down its circulation statistics to such commonly accepted divisions as general collection transactions, reserve book transactions, and periodical transactions; it simply records *total*

TABLE 22

SELECTED CIRCULATION STATISTICS FOR NINE UNIVERSITY LIBRARIES

University	F.T.E. Students	Total Loans	Loans Per F.T.E. Students	Salary Expenditures	Salary Expenditures Per Loan	Nonsalary Expenditures	Nonsalary Expenditures Per Loan	Total Expenditures Per Loan
A	9,570	231,447	24.2	$ 604,419	$2.61	$ 625,244	$2.70	$5.31
B	18,623	848,816	45.5	$ 845,092	$ .99	$ 435,607	$ .51	$1.50
C	11,906	713,053	59.8	$ 464,449	$ .65	$ 273,694	$ .38	$1.03
D	19,198	408,509	21.2	$ 459,080	$1.12	$ 440,559	$1.08	$2.20
E	29,299	756,164	25.8	$1,361,512	$1.79	$1,231,278	$1.63	$3.42
F	27,941	1,773,791	63.4	$2,505,870	$1.39	$1,948,886	$1.08	$2.47
G	6,089	129,172	21.2	$ 146,437	$1.13	$ 176,720	$1.36	$2.49
H	17,268	585,626	33.9	$ 447,457	$ .76	$ 396,707	$ .67	$1.43
I	26,834	2,414,918	93.7	$3,064,184	$1.22	$1,608,204	$ .66	$1.88
Median	18,623	756,164	33.9	$604,419	$1.13	$ 440,559	$1.08	$2.20

transactions. Three universities, representing a combined enrollment of over 40,000 students who responded to this writer's 1965-66 survey, are not recorded in Tables 22 and 23 because none keep circulation statistics!

TABLE 23

HOME-USE LOANS FROM THE GENERAL COLLECTION OF ELEVEN UNIVERSITY LIBRARIES

University	F.T.E. Students	Home-Use General Collection Loans	Home-Use General Collection Loans per F.T.E. Student
A	9,570	139,670	14.7
B	18,623	330,046	17.7
C	11,906	171,469	14.4
D	19,198	349,357	18.2
E	29,299	410,956	14.3
F	27,941	1,046,517	37.4
G	6,089	57,732	9.5
H	17,268	267,423	15.4
J	1,552	15,692	10.1
K	16,561	96,078	5.8
L	17,403	252,939	14.5
Median	17,268	252,939	14.5

Table 23 is more in keeping with the type of surveys made of university libraries during the 1930's. It reveals that with but one notable exception the 12 books circulated per student on average per academic year reported by Harvie Branscomb for the first half of the century remains essentially the same. The home-use loans from the general collection reported in Table 23 is for a full *calendar* year—hence the 14.5 median reported on an academic year basis would compute out at about the 12 per *academic* year revealed by circulation statistics in years past. Does this mean that college students are reading about the same number of books as 40 to 50 years past? Likely the answer is no. Because of the surge of paperbacks not present in Branscomb's time it is more likely that students are reading a considerably larger quantity of books than times past—but in softcover format—yet maintaining the same level as decades past with respect to the reading of hardcover books. Moreover, it is a reasonable assumption that readers today *own* considerably more books than times past, due to newer methods of book manufacturing, resulting in the wide availability of low cost paperbacks.

Returning to Table 22, it is noteworthy that seven of nine universities surveyed in the Hostrop Study spent more dollars for salaries than for nonsalary expenditures (of which, moreover, capital outlay is excluded).

The disparity of *salary expenditures* per loan between institutions as shown in Table 22 is wide—from a low of 65¢ to a high of $2.61. *Non-salary expenditures* show a similar disparity with costs per loan ranging from 38¢ to $2.70.

Total expenditures per loan, representing the composite costs of university library operation, are remarkably diverse. From a low of $1.03 to a high of $5.31 represents an amount greater than a 500 percent difference in costs. It should also be pointed out that no one section of the country has lower operating costs per loan than another. Moreover, size of institution does not correlate in any statistically significant way with loan costs. In short, it is institutional *philosophy and policies* concerned with a university's library operation, and to a much larger extent its *teaching methodology*, which determine what the costs per loan will be. However, in so far as how the library budget is divided between salary or nonsalary categories teaching methodology has little influence. That determination is made almost entirely by the library administrator.

It seems evident from the figures reported in Tables 22 and 23 that the wide disparity between universities cannot be attributed largely to differences in teaching procedure and methodology. The university, above all other types of institutions of higher education, has been noted for its dependence on the lecture method. What accounts for the differences reported much more likely can be attributed to (1) method and policy for reporting circulation statistics, (2) accessibility and ease of borrowing library-media materials, and (3) fund allocations between salary and nonsalary categories by the library administration.

Conclusion

If the American Library Association, in its annual *Survey of College and Universities,* would include in its survey form several items pertaining to circulation, a valuable self-evaluation tool would be readily accessible. So that meaningful comparisons and determinations of circulation trends can be achieved, the ALA would have to agree on (1) standard definitions of circulation terms, (2) what loans to include in the survey form, and (3) the method for counting and recording these loans. The literature is rampant with excuses by college and university library administrators as to the "meaningless" of recording circulation—yet most every library informally keeps such statistics now as the 1965-66 Hostrop study has revealed. Though several universities in the 1965-66 Hostrop Study keep no circulation statistics whatsoever, *all* universities reported in Tables 22 and 23 keep *year-to-year* circulation statistics. Moreover, most of these university library administrators include in annual reports to their university central administrators information on how their circulation statistics compare from one year to the next, as well as setting forth a brief analysis of circulation trends. Circulation statistics, above all other criteria, justify the library-media budget. When one institution spends considerably more dollars per loan than another institution, certainly that institution should want to determine the why of the disparity.

National figures, compiled and summarized by the ALA, would make it possible for individual institutions to compare their loans per student, costs per loan, their distribution of salary to nonsalary expenditures with the national figures. Such revelations could lead to increased efficiencies and service. Widely disparate results from the mean and/or median might lead to a change of L-MC philosophy and policy—a change designed to lead to greater ease at getting to and checking out library-media materials by the user. It may cause a reverse in expenditures with more of the budget going into materials. It might result in greater dependence on paraprofessional and technical library-media workers instead of on professional librarians. At any rate, it is time for library-media administrators in *every* type of institution to correlate their loans with the population served and to determine what the costs per loan are so as to achieve greater service and cost efficiencies.

Such research findings and conclusions as cited above can serve as an aid to future and present practitioners with respect to how self-studies and correlated national studies can be used to provide better service and cost efficiencies. Research into library practices is not to be feared. On the contrary, research can serve as an important self-evaluation tool which can aid in doing a better job.

There will be an increasing demand for research for there are strong winds of change indicating that before the year 2000, the entire antiquated structure of credits, majors, and degrees may be a shambles. No two students will move along exactly the same educational track. Destandardization will be the norm. With destandardization, and its concomitant diversity, there will be no choice but for the college library to be transformed into a learning center—having diverse multi-media learning materials and services available which are unheard of today. Critical self-study through research and evaluation will result in accountable structures to meet the complex learning needs of a diverse society in the 21st century. The trend is for the academic library to become a "library-college."

THE LIBRARY-COLLEGE CONCEPT

The whole universe is your Library: Authors, conversation, and remarks upon them, are your best tutors— Anon

Many consider the *Library-College* movement to be the most exciting and worthwhile development occurring in the library-media field. L-C "heretics" are on the cutting edge of what the profession, as a whole, will most likely be doing a decade hence.

Previous chapters have suggested various methods and means of implementing the Library-College concept. Such methods and means, though, were not labeled as being examples of the Library-College concept. Before we proceed it should be noted that "library" and "college" are hyphenated: "Library-College." This deliberate hyphenation is to emphasize that the library *is* the college and the college *is* the library; they are one. Certainly, it would also be appropriate to substitute the word "college" in "Library-College" with "school" to read "Library-School" meaning that the library *is* the school (elementary, junior high school, senior high school) and the school *is* the library. In short, the concepts set forth in this chapter and earlier in chapter 2 are universally applicable to all levels of education—they vary only to the degree of experience and maturity of the learner.

Library-College is a concept which presupposes that more effective student learning will result when instruction is library-centered, when the study mode is individualistic, and the faculty is comprised of bibliographically-minded teachers and subject-based librarians.

Louis Shores is generally credited with crystalizing previous thinking on the Library-College concept. Dean Shores defines Library-College thusly in the preface of his *Library-College USA* (South Pass Press, 1970):

> . . . The Library-College is a very special kind of college, and a very special kind of library. Its college individuality is in its *learning mode.* The uniqueness of its library is the concept of the *Generic Book.* . . .
> The Library-College *learning mode* reverses the traditional relation-

ship of classroom-library to library-classroom. Instead of going to classes regularly, and visiting the library irregularly, as time permits, the Library-College I favor advocates regular, student independent study in the library, at his individual workbench, we call a carrel; 'wet,' if possible, or as 'damp' as finances and technology will permit. . . .

In this learning mode the faculty role is almost as reversed as is the student's. Instead of meeting a class at regular hours, the instructors hold irregular class or group meetings as the occasion demands or suggests. . . .

. . . the high art of the . . . teacher becomes the sensitive matching of individual differences in his students with individual differences in media. . . .

. . . the *Generic Book* can be defined as *the sum total of man's communication possibilities.* It includes all media *formats, subjects,* and *levels.* Under this definition, a 16 mm motion picture is just as much of a book as, for example, a collection of 32 or more pages of paper, bound or loose leaf, consisting of printed reading matter or illustrations. . . . Other formats of the *Generic Book* include filmstrips, and transparencies; discs, tapes, radio transcriptions and videotapes; community resources—natural, social, human; programmed materials—print, machine, and computer assisted, as well as all kinds of print, and other sensory and even extrasensory media. . . .

The Library-College recognizes the fact that one learner may learn better a particular fact, principle, or theory from a printed page; another student from a time-lapse motion picture; a third from a videotape; a fourth from a transparency overlay. Nor does it forget the level of maturity of the student, with which librarians and teachers have long been concerned. And, of course, the librarian through his classification systems has been as conscious of subject as has his classroom faculty colleagues operating under the strict discipline boundaries of curricula and learned societies. Consequently, Library-College library book selection is three-pronged: subject, level, format, throughout.

It can thus be understood from Dean Shores' explanation of "Library-College" that the emphasis of this concept is on the student being responsible not to the limited requirements of a specific subject or course, but to the entire range of the subject matter of the field being studied.

In the Library-College concept, the faculty is comprised of bibliographical-ly-minded teachers and subject-based librarians. Photo courtesy of Prairie State College.

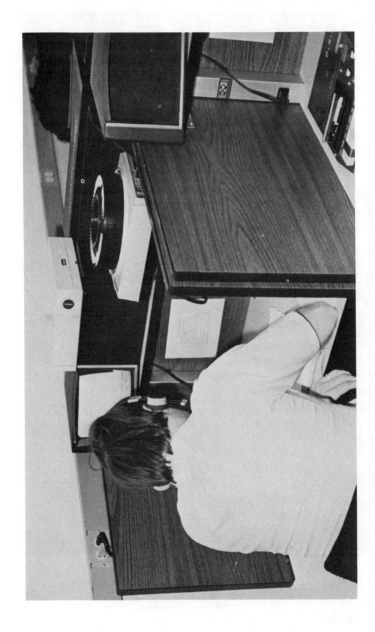

The Library-College concept presupposes that more effective student learning will result when instruction is library centered. Photo courtesy of Prairie State College.

And as Sister Marie Schuster, Librarian of Mary College in Bismarck, North Dakota, has pointed out in *Mary College Weekly Bulletin* (Jan. 29, 1971):

> . . . By encouraging the student to become immersed in the literature of the subject, Library-College aims to provide for the development of a student's critical discernment, independent judgment and ability to evaluate, not to inculcate a deference to the authorities that have been set up. The Library-College idea is to make the student more responsible for his own education and to assure him a greater measure of independence in pursuing it. This necessitates an adjustment of the program to the differences which exist between individual students. For years educators have claimed that they have been adjusting the educational program to individual differences, but a realistic look at the educational program causes the credibility gap to widen as one sees classes of 15, 25, or even 50 unique persons being subjected to the same text, the same lectures, the same reserve books, and the same discussions. Library-College emphasizes learning, not teaching, and in fact holds that you cannot teach anyone anything, you can only provide an opportunity to learn. And learning means developing the ability to think, to judge, to evaluate; it does not mean acquiring an assortment of facts or views. Finally, Library-College characterizes the educated individual as one who is inquisitive, has intellectual initiative, and is independent in his thinking. The educated individual is not necessarily one who possesses a degree.

Dr. Howard Clayton, Editor of *Learning Today,* and of the School of Library Science at the University of Oklahoma, though not the originator of the Library-College concept, has come to be known as one of its foremost and eloquent spokesmen. Dr. Clayton, in an address at the sixth Library-College conference held in Chicago in 1969, made a number of observations which will aid the reader still further in grasping the Library-College concept.

Dr. Clayton pointed out that a good education consists of (1) developing those abilities which will lead to independent judgment, (2) developing decision-making ability which will lead to economic efficiency, and (3) developing the senses in order to have a more meaningful life. The Library-College concept, acknowledges that the learner must be given the opportunity to pick and choose from the whole range of knowledge—not just from a lecture in which "the teacher is the big bottle and the 30 students are 30 little bottles into which his big bottle is poured."

The Library-College concept argues against the single lecturer and the single textbook—even against reserve books set aside in the library. Reserve books, like textbooks, represent assigned reading. While this may be a step above the textbook, if nothing is studied except assigned reading then education remains indoctrination rather than becoming elucidation. Library-College advocates espouse the Generic Book so that students are exposed to all ranges and kinds of knowledge bearing on a given subject. The concept stresses responsible learning—not teaching with its emphasis on memorization and regurgitated feedback on tests. It is much easier to memorize than to think but to think is the greater virtue.

A student who is *taught* acquires the ability to effectively listen to the predigested solutions of others (the lecturer) which results in a memorizer rather than a learner. On the other hand, a student who has *learned* will be able to relate the knowledge of the discipline he has acquired throughout life. The first may be enough to get a degree but it will not produce a sensitive human being.

The true learner is personified by the "little old man" who uses the public library. Though we consider the Little Old Man "odd," he represents an "ideal" in that he comes to the library not because he has to do an assignment but because he is motivated by the sheer joy of learning what he wants (and perhaps needs) to learn. In sum, learning how to independently learn is the most important skill a student can learn while in school and college. Indeed, Winslow Hatch has declared, "The degree to which a student can study independently is a measure of quality education."

If the goal setters of education are truly interested in having their products (graduates) acquire awareness, self-actualization, and the "good life," then increased emphasis is needed on quality, beauty, and thought. In short, graduates should *want* to go on learning broadly in these areas. Someone once said, "You know, the trouble with students is that they become alumni!" Perhaps if we abandoned graduations greater emphasis on life-long learning would result. Graduation is not the end of learning, though many of us act as though this ceremony symbolizes just that.

The Library-College movement, with its individualized learning mode and utilizing the Generic Book, encourages a student to proceed at his own rate, in his own way, and on his own level of intellectual ability. How much better this approach is than the established way in which emphasis is on teaching, the textbook, and recall tests with the inherent leveling characteristics of this approach.

Research has revealed that there is a low correlation between what a college coerces a learner to learn and that what he subsequently chooses to learn on his own. Moreover, extensive research by the American Council of Testing has revealed that *there is no correlation between grades earned and later success in life* no matter how success is defined (other than "academic success" per se!). The implications of these two facts argue strongly in favor of the implementation of the Library-College concept at all levels of the educational ladder.

Because teaching and learning are *not* synonomous we need to study the *science* of learning—not the *art* of teaching. In the L-C mode the audiovisualist, the librarian, and the teacher, each complementally fused to the other, become (1) a learning theorist, (2) a designer of instructional systems, (3) a manager of the instructional systems and program, (4) a facilitator of a broad range of learning paths, (5) a tutor and bibliographer, (6) a participant with the learner in certain learning paths, (7) a counselor for students, faculty, audiovisualists and librarians—each to the other, (8) a director and manager of facilities and learning resources. What the foregoing means, of course, is that the role of the audiovisualist, librarian and the teacher more nearly merge into one. One day, they may merge nearly or completely.

Those L-M technologists associated with the L-C movement are considered to be the "heretics" of the multi-media profession—in fact they really do not like to think of themselves as audiovisualists, librarians or as library-media workers per se but rather as "interdisciplinarians." Though those associated with the L-C movement currently outnumber "nonlibrarians" there are a significant number involved in the movement who have never taken a single course in audiovisual education or in library science.

This is not surprising, nor will it be surprising that the membership in the Library-College Association consists of more "nonlibrarians" than library-media professionals per se, since the movement is concerned with determining and implementing those methods and means which best facilitate learning. Undoubtedly, this will require a different kind of preparation program for both library-media professionals and faculty. It may be that in the future *all* those associated with the teaching-learn-

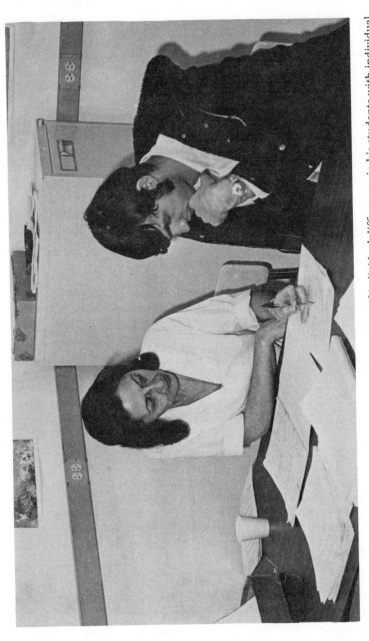

The high art of the teacher becomes the sensitive matching of individual differences in his students with individual differences in media. Photo courtesy of Prairie State College.

ing process will be *faculty*. The "New Faculty" will possess both an academic *and* a learning skill specialty. New Faculty will form into teams of professionals and paraprofessionals who will work closely together with students to aid them in their search for self-realization.

This chapter concludes with a *Charter for the Library-College* which will aid the reader in further understanding the education, learning, and intrinsic development of human beings as advocated by L-C proponents. Moreover, those readers wishing to follow the L-C movement more closely may readily do so through the Association's publications, *Learning Today* and *The Library-College Omnibus* (Box 956, Norman, Oklahoma 73069).

A Charter for the Library-College
(Adopted by the Workshop on the "Library-College" Jamestown College, Jamestown, North Dakota. December 19, 1965)

The purpose of the Library-College is to increase the effectiveness of student learning, particularly through (though not limited to) the use of library-centered, independent study with a bibliographically expert faculty. This charter assumes that the "library-college concept" can and should be adapted to colleges with varying objectives and philosophies. The curriculum of a particular library-college must emerge from its objectives and philosophy.

I. Library-centered, independent study with a bibliographically expert faculty requires:

A. Library materials: As conceived in this statement, library materials represent varying points of view and typically include the following organized for independent use:

1. Reference sources representing knowledge in all pertinent fields.
2. The Good Books (basic editions of the great monuments of human thought—the time-tested classics).
3. Representation of the better current literature in all pertinent fields, including hardcovers, paperbacks, serials, etc.
4. Graphics (maps, globes, charts, pictures, dioramas, realia, etc.).
5. Projections (transparencies, slides, film strips, microfilms).
6. Transmissions (disc, tape, radio, TV).
7. Resources (human, social, natural).
8. Mechanical, automated, electronic, computer, programmed and other "new educational media."

B. Independent study: Independent study with faculty assistance
will typically include:
1. Definition of goal or problem.
2. Selection of methods of study or investigation.
3. Conduct of study or investigation.
4. Report of findings.
5. Evaluation of findings.
C. Bibliographically expert faculty: The faculty will be expert in
knowing:
1. Library materials as defined in A (above) in their respective
fields.
2. How to use library materials as defined in A (above) as
vehicles of learning in their respective fields.
D. Students at Library-College: Students at the Library-College will
be expected to achieve competence:
1. In reading, writing, speaking, and listening.
2. In critically using resources of learning (including library materials defined in A (above) in independent study and investigation.
3. In intelligently relating these resources to the educational objectives and philosophy of the particular college in which they
are enrolled.

II. Library-centered, independent study, with a bibliographically expert
faculty, will typically—though not invariably—require:
A. Abundance of appropriate library materials as defined in I.A.
(above)
B. Merging of present library and classroom teaching functions in
the same individual—the new breed faculty member.
C. Library facilities which appropriately permeate the campus.
D. Varied syllabi, bibliographies, and reading guides.
E. Abundance of activity related to varying views on controversial
ideas and issues.
F. Cooperative exploration, discovery, and synthesis by faculty and
students rather than perpetuating a "master-disciple" relationship.

III. Since life is broader than library-centered, independent study, students in the Library-College will have planned experience in other
and varied aspects of living. To this end in the Library-College,
library resources will be used as much as possible to enrich such
activities as the following, these to be selected on the basis of the
objectives and philosophy of any given college:

A. Worship and meditation.
B. Participation in the fine arts.
C. Conducting scientific and other experiments.
D. Participation in discussions, forums, and lectures.
E. Participation in citizenship and community service.
F. Participation in the practical arts.
G. Participation in recreation and social activities.
H. Engaging in field work.

A LOOK AHEAD

The future will unfold as an unending succession of bizarre incidents, sensational discoveries, implausible conflicts, and wildly novel dilemmas—Alvin Toffler

The dimly perceived future of what knowledge making, storage, transmission and learning may become is suggested below. One thing seems certain: the knowledge industry which already accounts for 35 percent of the United States' gross national product will not become less. Rather, it is likely to increase in the decades ahead. The enormity of the educational enterprise is brought home by the fact that the U.S. Office of Education reported that in 1972 sixty-one million persons attended classes and ninety billion dollars was spent on education. Enrollments and costs point upwards in all parts of the world. The world of the year 2000 can only be dimly glimpsed. But one thing is certain—it will be different than it is today.

The importance of examining the revolutionary trends in the knowledge industry is plain. If we focus on present practices we will become obsolete by the time present practices can be mastered. In short, we need to continually train and prepare ourselves for the future that soon will be ours. By looking ahead, we condition ourselves to the inevitability of exponential change. By so doing, we will be masters of our fate rather than being mastered by fate.

Before this book can be published there will have been new developments on the educational horizon barely glimpsed by but a small handful. Therefore much of what is reported in this final chapter, although futuristic in focus, may have become present and past within but a short span of years, weeks, or in some instances even days! Let us examine some of the changes expected.

Miniaturization will accelerate at an ever increasing rate. And with it, radical changes will occur in the Library-Media Center. A United Press International article written in May 1971 was headlined "Future libraries may shun books." Reporting the statement of John R. Robertson, a micrographic expert for Eastman Kodak Co., it stated: "The library may very well be a computer-run storehouse with on-the-spot Microfilm printout as the sole source of loanout material." Such statements may seem revolutionary, but they are not new for people have been talking about them for a long time. However the technology has advanced so rapidly in recent times that the new era may indeed be upon us.

Like other technological advances in the communications field, the great change in media information storage and retrieval has come through miniaturization. What the transistor is to radio and television, high reduction photography is to the printed page. By photographing materials at very great reduction a small, transparent film card called a microfiche can contain a whole book. With advanced technology, however, it is now possible to print six books on a single 3"x5" card. Whereas the ordinary microfiche contains sixty to a hundred page-images per card, the new process of ultra-super-microfiche can pack a thousand page-images into this space, arranged in fifty columns and twenty rows.

One of the most striking results of this development is what Encyclopedia Britannica, Inc., calls a "Microbook Library." The advantages are obvious. It will cost L-MCs only a fraction of the normal price to buy a large collection of books, which can then be stored in a far smaller space; more than 250 microbook cards fit into the space occupied by a regular volume. Drastic cost reduction and major spacesaving: these have been the dreams of librarians for a long time.

Britannica's Library of American Civilization, 20,000 volumes numbering about six million pages sells for $21,000. If all the titles included were available for purchase as bound books they would cost about $450,000. These volumes would normally require 2,000 feet of shelf space; in super-microfiche format they require only thirty-two small card trays, 16 inches long. Not only are future Microbook Libraries planned in medieval civilization, English literature, African studies, international affairs, the history of science and technology, and the history of philosophy and religion, but some other publishers such as the University of Toronto Press are beginning to publish titles in both standard book format and on microbook cards simultaneously.

The development of excellent retrieval hardware, although slower than the technology of micro production is becoming increasingly available at an accelerated reduction in costs. Another development is the reader-printer that makes hard-copy printouts of any microbook page. However, the sorting out of the enormous copyright problems involved remains to be settled.

Another new development is the National Cash Register Company's process called *Ultramicrofiche,* or, more conveniently, UMF. One of these cards is capable of carrying 3,200 pages. The UMF of NCR will also have libraries to be sold under the general title of the PCMI Library Information System. One PCMI ultramicrofiche carries the equivalent of seven to ten books. An accompanying reader-printer features a screen about the size of a portable television set onto which is projected an image larger than the original. Touching a button produces on the printer a page reproduction of excellent quality in ten seconds. PCMI's collections will cost L-MCs about $1.50 per volume. A L-MC subscribing to PCMI pays $6,000 for full service, which includes one machine, 3,500 books on cards, and a set of catalogue cards. NCR already has put 6,000 books on ultramicrofiche; it expects to have 50,000 volumes stocked in five years.

Still another development of more than ordinary significance is the creation of *The New York Times'* Information Bank, which the newspaper put into operation in 1971. The *Times* calls it "the first fully automated system for the retrieval of general information." With this computerized system, the *Times* makes available to the general public the tremendous collection of information contained in its files.

Involved in the system is a complex of IBM computers, a high-speed printer, a microfiche storage and retrieval device controlled by another computer, and both video screen and hard-copy printer terminals. This bank stores all news and editorial matter from the *Times,* as well as a selection of material from more than sixty other newspapers and periodicals. Detailed abstracts of this material, along with index terms and other necessary elements, are stored in the computers. The full text of this material, including illustrations, is stored in an automated retrieval device. Users can view both the abstracts and the full text on video screens, and obtain printouts of either if they like, provided they do their viewing at the *Times,* where usage will be primarily for staff members. Those outside see only the abstracts at terminals in subscribing public libraries, but they are able to get a full set of microfiche material and a reader-printer as well. Using the references given in the abstract, it is easy to find the proper fiche for viewing or reproducing.

The system includes items selected from the millions of clippings in the paper's morgue, and these are fed into the computers as fast as is technically possible. In the future, the system will be expanded to include photographs and other graphic materials, besides bibliographic citations of books and reference materials in the *Times* library. Eventually, technology will permit the *Times* bank to be used in conjunction with other computerized information systems.

Obviously, the *Times* bank is of exceptional value to major reference and research libraries, a variety of businesses, and individuals engaged in many kinds of research, as well as writers, scholars, and journalists. In this system, the wave of the future is clearly discernible. Users will be sitting at video or typewriter terminals and will type out "descriptors" that define the question they want to ask. After a dialogue with the system, in which the terms can be connected by "and," "or," or "but not" in order to define the limits of the search, the bank will be put into operation and produce abstracts of what is needed on the screen, from 4″x 6″ pieces of microfiche film holding ninety-nine images each. The response time will take on the average only a few seconds. Outside customers will get printouts from the *Times* on request, or at the terminals they are using, if equipped with a printing capability. The familiar *New York Times Index* will no longer be a separate operation, but will be a subsystem of the Information Bank. People will still be able to write the paper requesting information, but generally they will be given only bibliographical citations, that is, title, date, page, and column.

When the system begins, data will be fed into it every day, supplementing the tapes from the index that were first put into the computer in January 1968. The earlier material, drawn from the paper's twenty million clippings, will be fed in gradually.

Data banks, about which so much has been theorized for so long, are plainly becoming a reality as far as printed materials are concerned. What is being done for books and newspapers has been accomplished for periodicals. University Microfilms, a subsidiary of the Xerox Corporation, has indexed about thirty-five periodicals and has fed this information into a data bank. The company produces semiannual indexes of this literature, which can be printed out from information in the bank. The index includes title, author, and five or six subject headings crossreferenced. There are separate listings for poems, films, books, and other categories. Wherever pssible, subject headings are adapted to individual disciplines. In chemistry, for example, terms used are indigenous to the field but with cross references for the layman. Periodicals indexed cover a broad spectrum. Eventually, there will be from a hundred to 150 periodicals in the data bank.

Although microfiche and microbooks will make their initial impact on L-MCs, home uses are easily foreseen. It is a development that cannot come too quickly for the nation's hard-pressed L-MCs, struggling against space limitations and inadequate budgets. There is a new book selection and acquisition system, developed by Bro-Dart Industries, called "direct input ordering." A single roll of microfilm, capable of being updated on a regular basis, will provide librarians with the details of more than 350,000 books. On microfilm viewers, librarians will be able to easily and rapidly look up titles, recording and transmitting their orders by means of a self-checking order code that will save both time and clerical expense. It will mean substantial savings in the ordering process.

Yet another much-heralded development is the cassette video player as applied to books. Those who have been thinking of it only in terms of visual entertainment, or as a supplement to television, may be surprised by this more immediately feasible application.

Early in 1971, Motorola EVR teleplayers were installed in a hundred of the nation's 27,000 L-MCs. Total cost of the project was $3,350, and each L-MC bought a teleplayer and a hundred titles, including documentaries in the arts and sciences and contemporary social problems. The players cost about $87 each, and black-and-white cassettes sell for $27 for a fifty-minute program. The films were selected from the National Audio-visual Center's archives in Washington.

In reporting this development, *Media Industry Newsletter* gives much of the credit for its initiation to Mrs. Joan Clarke, films and recordings consultant to the New York State Public Libraries, who foresaw the potential of video cassettes in L-MCs as early as 1967. She talked to manufacturers and discovered that not one of them had thought of the L-MC as potential customers. They were concerned only with industrial and home entertainment uses. She chose Motorola because it had the only system with players immediately available. L-MCs don't care about specific technology, Mrs. Clarke argued; they only want a system that works.

"We couldn't have cared less if the sound and film came out of a jukebox or an eggbeater," the *Newsletter* quotes her. "Some sort of cassette system was the logical step for libraries, which have, after all, progressed from clay tablets to parchment scrolls to printed materials to phonograph records and 16 mm films. Schools and fraternal organizations are about the only ones who borrow films. How many people have a 16 mm projector at home?" Mrs. Clarke believes that the teleplayer will be standard in American homes and that the demand for library cassettes will surpass that for books.

Occasionally, a word of caution is heard. Reviewing the development of L-MCs and information centers Gerard Salton, professor of computer science at Cornell, argues that "the first order of business must not be the introduction of new equipment and methodology but rather a re-evaluation of the aims and standards of the library in the modern world." Professor Salton also thinks it unlikely that the present convenience of handling books and journals by hand can be matched very soon by other devices.

Whether or not the L-MCs reevaluate their aims and standards, it is clear that technology is catching up to both L-MCs and readers so rapidly that things are never going to be the same again.

As miniaturization of transistors and other elements and materials proceeds, the resultant effect on knowledge transmission, and those who control this transmission, will be dramatic.

What seems likely is that the classroom of the future will be the entire library-campus. There will not be the egg-crate classrooms that we now know. There will be seminar rooms and large lecture halls. But for most, the individual wet carrel for each student will have replaced the class-room. The individually assigned carrels will be located in large mall areas, surrounded by an abundance of print and nonprint materials.

The carrels will retrieve 3-D color holographic sound images through coded programs wired in to a regional educational computer.

Because teachers cannot teach anyone anything—only the learner can learn—the teacher's role will become that of program designer, learning facilitator, discussion leader, and learning manager. In short, teachers will acquire many of the skills of audiovisualists and librarians. Conversely, audiovisualists and librarians will become more like teachers (and more like each other). Roles will converge—yet each will maintain some distinction—albeit blurred.

The school, then, of the future will be a L-MC. All the trends of the present point to independent study by the student as the dominant pattern of American education. Group teaching in a classroom is relentlessly being subordinated to individual learning in a carrel. The faculty is lecturing information less and guiding bibliographically more. And that part of the faculty called "audiovisualists" and "professional librarians" is more willing than ever to let clerks and automation take over management and housekeeping chores, so that at long last mediaship may devote itself to its chief purpose—education. What is emerging, inevitably, then is the trend toward independent study with concomitant role modification by both students and generic faculty.

Up to recent times the independent-study movement was a phenomenon reserved for the superior student—"the upper 10%" who had inherited the intellectual talents labelled educationally as "gifted." This is beginning to change. Happily, the change seems to be accelerating at a geometric rate.

Six elements of knowledge transmission of the future include: (1) Learning Mode; (2) L-MC; (3) Faculty; (4) Curriculum; (5) Facility; (6) Organization. A discussion of each follows.

The Learning Mode

Of the learning mode enough has been said to emphasize the locus shift from group-teaching in the classroom to individual learning in the L-MC carrel. The philosophy of this mode was well put for Bennington College when education was conceived as "intellectual adventure rather than indoctrination," and the college bulletin announced as a principal aim "to accustom its students to the habit of engaging voluntarily in learning rather than submitting involuntarily at certain periods to formal instruction."

The student learns primarily by "reading." This is not unlike the English university where the student records not that he is attending a class in psychology but rather that he is "reading" in psychology, or in chemistry or in philosophy, or Spanish, or whatever. Although a major part of this reading is done in the format known as "hardcover," the "new" faculty guides and encourages students to study in all formats. Such reading may include listening to tapes and discs; viewing transparencies, filmstrips, motion pictures; listening and viewing radio, television, VTRs, holograms, and the entire repertoire of educational media formats; it may, indeed, enlist sensory-experiencing with all of the five senses. To quote *Saturday Review*'s Frank G. Jennings:

> But reading, remember, is not restricted to the printed page. Actually it never was . . . throughout his history man has "read" many things: the flight of birds, the guts of sheep, sun spots, liver spots, and the life lines on a hand. He has read the lore of the jungle, the spoor of the beast and the portents in a dish of tea. But whatever he has read and however he has read, it has always been for "reason."

In short, reading encompasses the generic book in all of its formats. In the course of his academic life the student's reading will add up to all of the sensory responses to his environment.

But the student is also learning by doing, by demonstrating, by performing, by manipulating, and by speaking, writing and teaching. One
measure of an educated man or woman is the ability to communicate.
The student will write as well as read. He will write well and frequently—
reports, papers, essays and even imaginative literature, including poetry.
He will speak informally in conferences with faculty and fellow students,
with continuous, conscious and critical effort to improve the form of
his speech and add a creative element to it.

The student will strive to do the many things required to maintain life.
Part of each day will be devoted to perfecting himself in the tasks of
homemaking and earning a living. The student will perform in any of
the arts he selects: music, the dance, sculpture, painting, architecture.

Now the least "formal" student performing opportunity is the "each
one teach one" learning procedure. Toward the end of the 18th century
two English educators, Andrew Bell (1753-1832) and Joseph Lancaster
(1778-1838) each claimed to have originated the "monitorial" system
of instruction under which advanced students drilled their juniors in
fundamentals. In recent years this system has been used by the mission-
ary Dr. Laubach to advance literacy in backward nations. The advantage
of this system is mutual to both monitor and learner. Every one who
has ever taught will affirm that knowledge is reenforced by the teaching
of it. The monitorial system is especially made-to-order for an independent
study program. The 18th century mode may reemerge into a more sophisticated 21st century form.

The L-MC

The L-MC is, to paraphrase Carlyle, primarily a collection of books.
But the book is the generic book. It includes a selection of every subject,
level and format pertinent to the educational mission. Levels will represent the range of individual differences in the student population of a
particular educational community. This could mean school-encyclopedia
level of science for some; post-graduate for others.

When it comes to format, the generic book, as it appears in Louis
Shore's book *Library-College USA,* is a beginning. There are at least a
hundred or more physical makeups of educational media found in the
schools and colleges of the nation. Representations of all or most of
them belong in the collection if only because one kind of format will
communicate better with the background of an individual student for a
particular learning situation. The form of the medium may influence
communication. Indeed it is entirely possible that format may change

meaning for different individuals. If this is so, then it is more important
than ever that the L-MC stock be representative of items in all formats.
Nor should so-called audio-visual media ever be considered non-book material, and therefore reduced in its educational status.

New dimensions of access to multi-media materials must be envisaged
in keeping with the materials themselves. The open stack is one must.
But so also is the recent extension of remote access. If the carrel is to become truly the student's work bench, the L-MC must be prepared to go
as far as possible from dry through damp to wet carrel. The wet carrel,
the reader will recall, is a carrel electrically equipped. It has dial access
to audio and visual material such as tape, disc, radio; to still projections
like transparencies, slides, filmstrips; to films, VTR and possibly to
closed circuit television, holograms, and remote console; to computer-
assisted instruction; to facsimile and radioteletype, etc. "Dampness"
represents various stages along the way from dry to wet carrels.

With regard to bibliographic access, we should look forward to the
computerized printout book catalog and microfiche as an eventual re-
placement for the card catalog. Present imperfections are only a delay.
We have reached the point where automation can now provide un-
limited instant-printout of index-bibliographies to any portion of the
collection, to any topic, and with many more analytics or descriptors
for each item than the standard five analytics on cards. In embryo, such
cataloging can be found at a number of colleges and universities: e.g.,
Florida Atlantic, Louisiana State at New Orleans, Missouri.

Besides the generic book stock, the L-MC will accomodate people.
These will include students, faculty and staff. For students, the first de-
parture will be to increase the percentage of student body seated at one
time from a conservative 25% beyond generous 50%, to 100%. This has
been done at Oklahoma Christian, where the present library seating
capacity is 110%. There will be an individual carrel for each student,
his individual work bench to which he can come at any time of the day
and night the L-MC is open. This does not prevent the student from
studying in his own room, if he prefers, with the radio on, or during a
conversation in progress between his roommate and a dropper-in; or in
the recreation room with every other sentence punctuated by a popping
ping pong. But he will also begin to live as he will after he leaves college
and has a place of work to report to daily. Nor will this prove architectural-
ly uneconomical when reckoned against unused class space-time. Already
classroomless schools and colleges exist—e.g., Oak View Elementary

School in Illinois, Oakland Community College in Michigan, and Governors State University in Illinois.

Faculty offices, one for each faculty member, will be in the L-MC. And for each four faculty offices there likely will be one seminar room. Faculty offices will be used for study, conference with colleagues and students.

Most of the special areas provided in the L-MC will be represented; public catalog and bibliography-index area; reference; current periodicals; browsing; rare materials; exhibits and displays. Equipment storage for projectors, recorders, playbacks, readers, etc., for use with the related formats of the generic book, as well as maintenance and service space areas, will be planned. Laboratory and demonstration space will be provided, although the Purdue experiment with its biological laboratory may point to the ideal accommodation for a laboratory in a library.

The Faculty

The new-breed faculty that will be required for the future is a cross between those audiovisualists and librarians who like to teach and those classroom instructors who like to use the L-MC in their teaching. There are enough of each today to provide a nucleus for the faculty of tomorrow's prototype. Essentially, this faculty member's job will be to guide bibliographically the great adventure in learning by the student. Inspirationally, the faculty member will arouse interest through about a half dozen carefully prepared lectures of such significance as to be worthy of public billing on the campus. He will stimulate by stirring discussion; through individual or small group conferences. Bibliographically, he will attempt to tailor media-selection to the individual differences of his students, prescribing much as the skilled medical diagnostician does.

To accomplish this, the faculty member will have to know media, not incidentally as he was taught them in his liberal arts or teachers college days, but *per se.* He will have to know his sources not alone for subject but for level. And above all he will have to know the strengths and weaknesses of the various formats for individual learning situations. For example, time-lapse motion pictures can accomplish communication of certain concepts better than almost any other medium. Yet there are some abstractions that cannot be mastered except by wrestling with the printed word. How better can a youngster gather the nuance of Spanish idiomatic conversation than through video cassette exchanges with high school or college students in Latin American countries? But what better way to understand Plato's *Dialogues* than by reading them in traditional print format?

The time is coming when orientation and teaching in library/media use will assume a new importance. With that will come a more creative approach to communicating this important half of knowledge—knowing what to use and where to find it. For the present, in-service education is called for. One device is for the faculty to undertake continuous index-ing of library materials for computerized retrieval much as is now carried on in scientific libraries. A thesaurus of descriptors, fields, and groups, based on units and terms in curriculum, could be used as a basis. And the librarian could lead the way by establishing a school or college-inter-est profile related to faculty research, to specialist and hobby interests. Likewise the audiovisualist could demonstrate new equipment, display nonprint knowledge materials, and demonstrate learning systems.

Prophetically, Carter Alexander anticipated the role of the faculty in this new and more exciting relationship to the student when he wrote, back in 1934:

> A plan must be developed . . . where the teaching process can be started and finished by the instructor and the learning process carried on effectively in the library . . . where suggestions can be given in the library as well as in the office of the professor.

Curriculum

"The curriculum is commonly defined," states the 1970 *Encyclopedia of Educational Research,* "as all the experiences that a learner has under the guidance of the school." Although the L-MC accents intellectual development, it by no means neglects "the effects upon learners of all aspects of the community, the home and the school." "Learnariums" of the future will periodically invite student diaries for review and ex-change, with the purpose of encouraging students to revise continuously the total experience planned.

Of the many statements of a liberal education aim, perhaps none fit the purpose of the L-MC better than the 1924 report by Professor Richardson to the President of Dartmouth College:

> . . . the stimulation and development of those gifts of intellect with which nature has endowed the student, so that he becomes, first,

a better companion to himself through life, and, second, a more
efficient force in his contacts with his fellow men.

To accomplish this purpose the future departs from the curriculum of
many contemporary liberal arts colleges by: (1) intellectually accenting
general background more, and specialism less; (2) physically and spiritual-
ly, converting elements of academic life formerly looked upon as "extra"
or "co" curriculum to an integral part of the curriculum, and (3) at least
an equal emphasis on the study of the future as on events of the past.

Curricula today suffer from the compartmentalization enforced by
the predatory rights and privileges of our contemporary academic disciplines. This will be overcome through the interdisciplinary approaches
of the Library-College mode. One approach to individualizing learning
is through the continuous building of a student-interest profile, covering
the range of interests of the student population, and becoming a continuous printout catalog. The student would pursue his studies in the individualized learning mode, working independently under the bibliographic guidance of the instructor. His studies would be along a continuous line stressing preparation for the needs of society in the future—not
the present. The knowledge trajectory of the future will become present
and past all too soon. Present studies indicate that, on average, today's
child will need to be retrained at least three times over a working period
of 40 years.

Future students will continue to consider the thoughts, actions, and
achievements that have most significantly been responsible for man's
present state. A beginning might be made through the "Good Books,"
a collection like the *Harvard Classics* or the *Great Books.* Added to these
would be the classics of the Eastern World. The student will be encouraged
to read across boundary lines, not only within the sciences, the social
sciences, and the humanities, as our now "old hat" integrated courses do
in most colleges, but across these broad areas, so that C. P. Snow's
doubtful accusation against the humanists might never be thought again
of a college graduate. Moreover, like the "classics," quality science fiction and futurist nonfiction will find a respected place in the future
curriculum. To prepare for the future man must study the future.

On the practical side, "New School" proposes to include, without
apology, in its curriculum: how to make a living, how to perform in the
world, how to get along with one's fellow men. Without particularizing
further, the curriculum has a place for such sacrilegious subjects (in the

opinion of the intellectualists) as marriage and the family, infant care; the ballet; intercollegiate football; farming; carpentry, etc.

And on the ethical side, there must be time for meditation. "Where the action is" apparently sells commercially. But if this nation is to be great it must begin to balance its national mind with more contemplation, with time to consider the ultimates. All of us know of the famous meditation room in the United Nations. Such meditation rooms must be provided for and encouraged in our New Schools.

Learning Facilities

The last word in L-MC architecture has yet to be written. As has been pointed out, likely it will be more like a shopping mall—but looking even further into the future it can be visualized where good-bye will not only be said to the classroom but the formal school building as well. Through electronics and miniaturization the dispersal may be so great that the home may become the chief center of learning. Only periodically will groups get together in formal learning sessions. It may be that the public library will in time replace school buildings entirely. Other community facilities could serve as places to have live lectures when needed—and to meet educational, recreational, and other needs.

But for the near future it can be expected that user-accommodation will depart from current L-MC building standards quantitatively by specifying that 100% of the student body be seated at one time. Qualitatively, the individual wet carrel rather than the group reading table will become standard. Typical designs for these carrels are available in such publications as the booklet issued by the *Educational Facilities Laboratory* office under the sponsorship of the Ford Foundation.

Staff-accommodation must provide offices for the new-breed of faculty; seminar rooms; and auxiliary bibliographic, browsing, reference, special format, and other work areas. Even though L-M professionals will now have merged with the classroom instructor to become the faculty, there will still be need to accommodate the management and housekeeping staff, probably according to the "100-foot per" standard.

Organization

For New School to function properly, enrollment should be limited to about 500. As enrollment increases on one campus, another school should be organized or a "house plan" formulated in which there are distinct schools within schools such as the University of California at Santa Cruz

plan. For a cluster of colleges, the university should perform certain resource and evaluation functions. Research and other expensive resources
which can be shared by all of the colleges will be housed in the university
library. All-university lectures by nationally and internationally distinguished
scholars will be open to all of the colleges. The university will act as an
evaluative agency for the programs of the various colleges, each of which
may have different accents. A federation of library-universities, therefore,
becomes library-university.

The organization of New School in elementary schools is best illustrated
by the English primary school on the one hand and the open classrooms
of North Dakota on the other. The secondary school model can best be
seen by the Parkway "school without walls" program in Philadelphia in
which learning primarily takes place in such places as offices, hospitals,
theaters, auto repair shops, banks, museums, and public libraries.

As we move beyond the twenty-first century it will be computers that
will store man's knowledge rather than academic libraries. Public libraries,
though, likely will emerge as the font of educational, social, and cultural
life in the community. But they will be unlike any library known today.

Beyond the twenty-first century a library user may be able to push a
button on his home information console for a no-deposit, no return
paperback printout, instead of standing in line to borrow a hardback
from the stacks. Today's books, by the year 2500, may become museum
pieces. Most likely, libraries will be on spools of computer tapes.

This has already begun at the University of Georgia at Athens. A staff
of 110 and computer hardware valued at more than $9 million provides
information. It works like this:

A professor sits before an apparatus that looks like the offspring of a
teletype machine and a television set. He types out the chemical name
of DDT on the keyboard. Then, almost in less time than it takes him to
peck out "dichloro-diphenyl-trichloroethane," the television screen above
the keyboard displays a list of 176 scientific references to DDT.

The information that flashes on the TV screen is the result of a lightning-
quick electronic search of about 40,000 issues of chemical abstracts, a
title compilation on computer tape of all published scientific papers in
chemistry. In addition to chemical abstracts, there are available abstracts
in biology, nuclear science, other chemical and biological indexes, and
listings found in the National Library of Medicine.

If sufficient funds were available, there would be practically no limit
to the knowledge that could be computerized. For example, it might be

possible to record the university's entire million volumes of library holdings on computer tape, and integrate it with computer information capability. Besides the perennial problems of time and money, there additionally will be the sticky problems to be worked out regarding copyrights and use royalties.

The information retrieval system allows a user to "browse as he would in a library," says Dr. Robert McRorie, director of general research at the university. But, the browsing is done through one of 37 remote terminals. The number of remote terminals to the center is expected to more than quadruple in future years, giving a total of some 200 individual outlets.

The geometric "explosion" of new knowledge, the accumulation of old information, and the proliferating of all forms of the arts, sciences, and culture make the job of becoming educated more difficult and more selective as time goes on. Electronic computers and memory storage devices will become the libraries and textbooks of tomorrow. Homes, businesses, classrooms, and individuals will all be "tuned in" on data banks and knowledge centers which will be tied into information networks on a national and international scale. Computerized knowledge centers become compulsory as we realize how finite we are with the awesome fact that we live with 90 percent of all the scientists *who have ever lived* and more than 90 percent of all the knowledge that *has ever been discovered!*

Teachers will be able to "tune in" on any picture, any experiment, or any book ever produced, and with a flip of a selector switch, may bring any part of the world onto a view screen. What better way to study Russia, other than going there, than via an electronic trip to its far reaches? With any part of the world within two hours of jetport, what will the field trip of tomorrow be like?

It is in this last mentioned great area of potential electronic applications that the social scientist, the L-M technologist, and the educator have much to ponder over. Probably the time will soon come when every individual will be assigned an electronic indentification number at birth.

Thereafter all information about him will be electronically gathered and stored, and related to his life, his eduation, his work, his experiences, and his family activities and avocational interests. This process could be good, and could help man to achieve maximum self-realization and education in the art of living as a supreme individual human being; or it

could be horribly bad, and could lead to state determined educational
goals, state evaluation of educational results of particular schools or
systems, and state supported and rewarded education for compliance
and, ultimately, the "robotization" and elimination of free men.

It's a challenging prospect, but we must have faith that men will find
a way to make electronics the servant, and not the master of his destiny!

In sum, unless we are in a continuing state of preparation, tomorrow's
world will have passed us by without our even having known it. It is
to be remembered that today's world was the world of the future for
those of yesterday. The library-media technologist who does *not* prepare for that tomorrow will be replaced by a machine—and ought to be.
The library-media technologist who *does* prepare for tomorrow can
never be replaced by a machine. He will be master of the machine and
it will be his servant. The wise use of these marvelous, miniaturized,
electronic servants will elevate the status of their masters.

Tomorrow's world is not to be feared. On the contrary, the excitement it holds, the service that can be provided, and the challenging
opportunities afforded are a part of tomorrow's world in which library-
media technologists can play an especially significant role.

The Boy Scout motto, "Be prepared" is an especially apt closing as
we begin to prepare the services demanded for the second millennium.

SELECTED BIBLIOGRAPHY
FOR FURTHER READING

BIBLIOGRAPHY

Abbott, J. C. "Co-ordination of Faculty Services," *College and Research Libraries,* XVII (January 1956), 13-15.

Allen, Kenneth. *Use of Community College Libraries.* Hamden, Conn.: The Shoe String Press, Inc., 1971.

American Library Association. Association of College and Research Libraries. Junior College Libraries Section. Standards and Criteria Committee. "Guidelines for Establishing Junior College Libraries," *College and Research Libraries,* XXIV (November 1963), 501-505.

——, ——, ——, ——. "Standards of Junior College Libraries," *College and Research Libraries,* XXI (May 1960), 200-206.

——. *Student Use of Libraries.* Chicago: The Association, 1964.

Bartlett, B. C. "Stephens College Library Instruction Program," *ALA Bulletin,* LVIII (April 1964), 311-314.

Bramley, Gerald. *History of Library Education, A.* Hamden, Conn.: The Shoe String Press, Inc. 1969.

Branscomb, Harvie. *Teaching with Books.* Chicago: Association of American Colleges, 1940.

Campbell, G. M. "Library Orientation for College Freshmen," *Library Journal,* LXXXI (May 15, 1956), 1224-1225.

Campbell, H. C. *Canadian Libraries.* Hamden, Conn.: The Shoe String Press, Inc., 1971.

Carpenter, Marjorie. "Building a Philosophy of Learning into a Library," *ALA Bulletin,* LV (February 1961), 173-176.

Clark, Burton R. *The Open Door College: A Case Study.* New York: McGraw-Hill Book Company, Inc., 1960.

Clark, Virginia. "Student Use of a Junior College Library," *Illinois Libraries,* XLII (1963), 316-318.

Delaney, Jack J. *Library Club, The.* Hamden, Conn.: The Shoe String Press, Inc., 1971.

Delaney, Jack J. *New School Librarian, The.* Hamden, Conn.: The Shoe String Press, Inc., 1968.

De Bono, Edward. *New Think.* New York: Basic Books, Inc., 1968.

Dimalanta, C. "Role of the Faculty Library Committee in Building the Collection and Improving Services in a College or Unit Library," *ASLP Bulletin,* VIII (March-June 1962), 11-14.

Dix, W. S. "Library Service to Undergraduate College Students; Under-
graduates Do Not Necessarily Require a Special Facility," *College and
Research Libraries*, XVII (March 1956), 148-150.

Draper, H. "Librarian vs. Scholar-User," *Library Journal*, LXXIX (May 1,
1964), 1907-1910.

Eurich, A. C. "The Significance of Library Reading Among College Students," *School and Society*, XXXVI (1932), 92 ff.

Footlick, Jerrold K. "Junior Colleges Fill Man-Sized Role in Education,"
National Observer (November 16, 1965), 11 ff.

Gaskill, H. V., R. M. Dunbar, and C. H. Brown. "An Analytical Study
of the Use of the College Library," *Library Quarterly*, IV (October
1934), 576.

Gerard, David E. *Libraries and the Arts*. Hamden, Conn.: The Shoe
String Press, Inc. 1970.

Green, Alan C., ed. *Educational Facilities with New Media*. Washington,
D.C.: Dept. of Audiovisual Instruction, N.E.A., 1966.

Green, Donald R. *Educational Psychology*. Englewood Cliffs, N.J.:
Prentice-Hall, Inc., 1964.

Harvey, J. F. "Role of the Junior College Library in Classroom Instruction," *Junior College Journal*, XXXII (April 1962), 441-447.

Hirsch, F. E. "Goals for the Nineteen-Sixties, the Significance of the
New ALA Standards for Junior College Libraries," *Junior College
Journal*, XXXI (November 1960), 135-139.

Hostrop, Richard W. *Teaching and the Community College Library*.
Hamden, Conn.: The Shoe String Press, Inc., 1968.

Johnson, B. Lamar. "New Junior College Library Standards—An Analysis and Critique," *ALA Bulletin*, LV (February 1961), 155-160.

———. *Vitalizing a College Library*. Chicago: American Library Association, 1939.

———, and Eloise Lindstrom, eds. *The Librarian and the Teacher in General Education*. Chicago: American Library Associaton, 1948.

Jones, R. C. "Use of the Library for Better Instruction," *Junior College
Journal*, XXIX (April 1959), 493-495.

Josey, E. J. "Role of the College Library Staff in Instruction in the Use
of the Library," *College and Research Libraries*, XXIII (November
1962), 492-498.

Joyce, W. D. "Student Grades and Library Use: A Relationship Establishe
Library Journal, LXXXVI (January 1961), 832-833.

Kast, G. E. "Unique Junior College Library," *Library Journal*, LXXXIII
(December 1, 1958), 3371-3372.

Knapp, Patricia B. *College Teaching and the College Library*. Chicago:
American Library Association, 1959.

———. *The Role of the Library in a Given College in Implementing Course
and Noncourse Objectives of That College*. Unpublished Ph.D. disserta-

tion, University of Chicago, 1957.

Knapp, Robert H., and Joseph J. Greenbaum. *The Younger American Scholar: His Collegiate Origins.* Chicago: The University of Chicago Press and the Wesleyan University Press, 1953.

Kneller, George F., ed. *Educational Anthropology: An Introduction.* New York: John Wiley and Sons, Inc., 1965.

Library-Instructional Integration on the College Level. Report of the 40th Conference of Eastern College Librarians, Held at Columbia University, November 27, 1954. ACRL Monographs, No. 13. Chicago: Association of College and Reference Libraries, 1955.

Mapp, Edward. "Instructor-Librarian Collaboration in a Community College," *Junior College Journal,* XXVIII (March 1958), 404-406.

Maxfied, D. K. "Counselor Librarians Stimulate Reading and Learning," *Improving College and University Teaching,* III (May 1965), 34-35.

McLuhan, Marshall. *Understanding Media.* New York: McGraw-Hill Book Co., 1964.

McCoy, R. E. "Automation in Freshman Library Instruction," *Wilson Library Bulletin,* XXXVI (February 1962), 468-470.

McDiarmid, Errett Weir, Jr. *Conditions Affecting Use of the College Library.* Unpublished Ph.D. dissertation, University of Chicago, 1934.

Medsker, Leland L. *The Junior College: Progress and Prospect.* New York: McGraw-Hill Book Company, Inc., 1960.

Merton, Robert K., and Patricia L. Kendall. "The Focused Interview," *American Journal of Sociology,* LI (May 1946), 541-547.

"Methodology and Results of the Monteith Pilot Project," *Library Trends,* XIII (July 1964), 84-102.

"Monteith Library Project, An Experiment in Library-College Relationship," *College and Research Libraries,* XXI (July 1961), 256-263.

Pratt, L. K. "Integration of the Junior College Library with Instruction," *College and Research Libraries,* XIX (May 1958), 201-202.

Rink, B. C. "Community College Library—Cultural Solar Plexus," *College and Research Libraries,* XXIII (September 1962), 389-392.

Shores, Louis. *Library-College USA.* Tallahassee, Florida: South Pass Press, 1970.

Stickler, Hugh W. *Experimental Colleges.* Tallahassee, Fla.: Florida State University Press, 1964.

Stieg, Lewis. "Circulation Records and the Study of College-Library Use," *Library Quarterly,* XII (January 1942), 94-108.

"Strengthening the College Library: ALA Standards for Junior College Libraries," *Improving College and University Teaching,* XII (Spring 1964), 87-90.

Student Use of Libraries. Papers of the Conference Within a Conference, July 16-18, 1963, Chicago, Illinois. A Feature of the 1963 American

Library Association Conference. Chicago: American Library Association, 1964.

Sutton, H. L. "Is the Library the Heart of the College?," *Saturday Review,* XLV (April 21, 1962), 42-43.

Tanis, N. E. "Co-operative Program to Improve the Community College Library," *Junior College Journal,* XXIX (March 1959), 405-411.

"Teaching Students to Use the Library: Whose Responsibility?," *College and Research Libraries,* XXI (September 1960), 369-372.

Toffler, Alvin. *Future Shock.* New York: Random House, 1970.

Trinkner, Charles L. *Better Libraries Make Better Schools.* Hamden, Conn.: The Shoe String Press, Inc. 1962.

Tyler, Leona E. *Psychology of Human Differences.* New York: Appleton-Century-Crofts, Inc., 1956.

Waples, Douglas, et al. *The Library.* Chicago: The University of Chicago Press, 1936.

Warner, W. Lloyd. *Social Class in America.* New York: Harper and Row, 1960.

Wheeler, Helen Rippier. *The Community College Library—A Plan for Action.* Hamden, Conn.: The Shoe String Press, Inc., 1965.

Wilson, Louis R., M. H. Lowell, and S. R. Reed. *The Library in College Instruction.* New York: The H. W. Wilson Company, 1951.

INDEX